T0352395

NEW CENTURY READERS

Seize the Fire

Notes: Pippa Doran

Edinburgh Gate
Harlow, Essex

Pearson Education Limited
Edinburgh Gate
Harlow
Essex
CM20 2JE
England

This educational edition first published 2002
Editorial notes   Pearson Education Limited 2002
20 19 18 17

ISBN 978-0-582-48852-6

Printed in Great Britain by Bell and Bain Ltd, Glasgow
GCC/12

Cover illustration by Matthew Williams

Contents

Introduction

About the authors
John Gordon: Under the Ice
John Gordon moved to East Anglia at the age of 12 and is a fine writer of horror and ghost stories. Many of his stories combine the supernatural with the everyday, creating unsettling and tense tales. *Under the Ice* is hauntingly set in the fens.

Robert Westall: Gifts from the Sea
The popular children's writer was born in 1929 in the north-east of England. Practically every teenager has read or heard of *The Machine Gunners*, one of Westall's most famous and well-loved books. Slightly less well known are his short stories that deal with the Second World War or supernatural themes, which are beautifully crafted and thought provoking.

Robert Swindells: Going Up
Robert Swindells was born in Bradford and worked as a teacher before becoming a full-time writer. He is not afraid to tackle difficult subjects in his novels and short stories, such as homelessness and drug abuse in *Stone Cold*. His story in this collection looks at peer pressure in gangs and has a surprising twist at the end.

James Berry: The Mouth-organ Boys
The Jamaican-born British writer has won many prizes for his poetry and stories for children and adults. Much of his work is set in the West Indies, Jamaica in particular, where he still spends a great deal of time when he isn't living in Sussex. His short stories are collected in *A Thief in the Village*.

Mary Hoffman: Seize the Fire
Mary Hoffman was born in Eastleigh, Hants. She has written over seventy books for children. Amongst her most famous books is the

bestseller, *Amazing Grace*, which has sold more than a quarter of a million copies in the United States. *Seize the Fire* is one of her engaging short stories and deals with the contemporary issue of conservation.

M. R. James: Rats

Montague Rhodes James was born in 1862. The head of King's College Cambridge, he also worked for the famous Fitzwilliam Museum. James authored nearly forty supernatural tales and his ghost stories remain popular to this day.

Sir Arthur Conan Doyle: The Speckled Band

The famous creator of the detective Sherlock Holmes was born in Edinburgh, Scotland, in 1859. He was influenced as a young medical student by his teacher Dr Joseph Bell, who made deductions about medical conditions from evidence, just like the detective Doyle later wrote about. By the end of his career Doyle had written sixty stories featuring Sherlock Holmes including *The Hound of the Baskervilles* and *A Study In Scarlet*.

Setting the scene

The title *Seize the Fire* has been given to this collection partly because of the excellent short story by Mary Hoffman included in the book, but also to indicate the lively and exciting nature of many of the stories. Their success lies in the immediacy of the writing, and the fact that a wide variety of subjects are tackled such as bullying, friendship, environmental and gender issues, to name but a few! The vocabulary and length of stories has been carefully monitored so that even the most reluctant reader will find stories that are interesting and relevant to them. Stories with a sports theme may interest boys particularly, although one of them has a surprising twist at the end which girls will definitely enjoy!

The range of genres in the collection not only covers some of the more difficult areas of the National Curriculum in English, such as pre-1914 literature, but will also allow you to discover or continue to investigate some of the principal writing genres in literature – science fiction, horror, suspense, humour – and introduce some newer ones like football stories. These excellent examples can be used as models for the writing process and there are a multitude of suggestions about how they can be used in the classroom. However, their main strength is simply that they are very good stories that grip the imagination and get children reading.

Main themes

There are many themes within these stories. To help both the pupil and teacher the stories have been grouped in pairs to encourage links with the reading objectives in the Framework, such as the investigation of the different ways familiar themes are explored and presented by different writers. In addition to this the organisation should assist the development of the comparative skills outlined in the orders for English and GCSE syllabi.

Ghosts (Under the Ice and Mayday!)

The contrasts in these two stories are striking. In *Mayday!* a ghostly pilot helps an old friend and saves the lives of all the people on the aircraft, whereas the ghost in *Under the Ice* takes his revenge on his supposed murderer, but also takes his murderer's innocent son into the frozen waters too.

War (Deserter and Gifts from the Sea)

Deserter and *Gifts from the Sea* give very interesting and thought-provoking views on war. In both stories the main characters initially have a mixture of feelings about war, ranging from pride to excitement. However, by the end of both stories events have brought them a whole new understanding of the effects of war.

Football (Charlotte's Wanderers and Going Up)

Football is the unifying subject of these stories. They are both written in the first person from a young person's point of view and because of that employ humour, use slang and have a lively style. Gender issues are also tackled in both stories. In *Charlotte's Wanderers* the football player is a young woman and her boyfriend has to fit in with her training and matches. In *Going Up* the young football supporter referred to as Tel is revealed to be a girl at the end of the story, a device reminiscent of *The Turbulent Term of Tyke Tyler* by Gene Kemp.

Relationships (*The Mouth-organ Boys* and *Fathers' Day*)
The Mouth-organ Boys shows an affectionate relationship between a son and his mother and, like *Going Up*, examines the effects of peer pressure on someone who is slightly outside a group. *Fathers' Day* shows a less successful relationship between a father and his son and sensitively examines masculine roles. Both these stories are also examples of excellent writing from other cultures.

Science Fiction (*Seize the Fire*)
This science fiction story offers a believable depiction of a future world, but also engages with contemporary themes such as conservation and the impact of virtual reality. Many teenage readers, both boys and girls, would identify with the daring actions of Toke.

Pre-1914 (*The Speckled Band* and *Rats*)
Both these stories have elements of mystery and suspense. Descriptions of places are extremely important in building up atmosphere. Dr Roylett's manor house and the inn are both very important settings where ghostly or murderous happenings take place. The historical background of both stories also adds extra detail which, unfortunately, can be a barrier to understanding for pupils. Ideas for looking at social and historical context as preparation for GCSE appear at the back of the collection.

Language and style
These rich and varied stories have very different styles, which are useful for exploring language choices with pupils and reinforcing

linguistic rules and conventions. There is a great deal of difference between the language used in the pre-1914 stories and, for example, *Going Up*, which deliberately uses slang and contemporary phrases to involve the reader. Also *The Mouth-organ Boys* and *Fathers' Day* show many examples of writing from another culture with different vocabulary and sentence structures, especially in conversation, and also highlight the differences between standard English and dialectal variations.

Five stories use a first-person narrative and the effects are very interesting. Dr Watson's telling of the Roylott mystery in *The Speckled Band* is very different to the teenager telling the story of his girlfriend's football team in *Charlotte's Wanderers*. This technique is extremely effective in involving the reader, whether by using humour or suspense.

The description of character is sometimes familiar and sometimes unexpected. Helen Stoner in *The Speckled Band* is a stereotypical weak Victorian woman and a powerless victim, and the story can help illustrate for pupils the culture in which it was produced. Conversely, Charlotte in *Charlotte's Wanderers* and Tel in *Going Up* show us how far modern, young women have been able to reverse portrayals of female characters into active, powerful roles. The way writers convey character through word choice and sentence structure can be investigated in the presentation of the violent Dr Roylett, the archetypal wicked stepfather in *The Speckled Band*. He contrasts sharply with the kind grandparents in *Gifts from the Sea*.

The pace of the stories is also very different making it possible to trace the ways in which a writer structures a text to prepare the reader for the ending. In *Under the Ice* the reader knows right from the beginning that something awful has happened, but in *Mayday!* everything appears to be going as normal at the beginning.

As previously mentioned, the settings of these stories are quite varied and intriguing. *Under the Ice* has a great deal of detail describing the eerie ice fields. The atmospheric setting of *Under the Ice* can also be compared with *Rats*, *The Speckled Band* and *Gifts from the Sea*. *The Mouth-organ Boys*, however, using much less descriptive language, conjures up a glowing, vibrant picture of life in the West Indies. The imaginative futuristic depiction of technology and places in *Seize the Fire* also grips the imagination.

SEIZE THE FIRE

Notes for Under the Ice

Summary

This unsettling story could be described as a ghost story or a horror story; either way it is not for the faint hearted! A teenage boy goes out skating with a friend in the bleak landscape of the fens, only to be caught up in a tale of family murder and revenge.

What do you think?

Right from the beginning of this story, the reader knows that something terrible has happened and that the narrator has seen a ghost. There are certain details which build up to create a sense of fear. As you read the story, think about the following:

- How is the countryside described? What effect does this have on the story?
- How are Rupert's parents described?
- What do you think has happened to Rupert's uncle and why?
- Can you explain the ending?

Questions

Choose words and phrases from the story to back up your answers.

1. Pick out phrases or sentences which suggest something awful has happened (for example 'I wish he'd kept quiet and then things might have turned out differently'). Explain what effect these phrases have on the story.

2. What sort of person is David? What is the effect of having him telling the story as a first-person narrator?

3. How does Rupert react to seeing the body under the ice? Why do you think he has shown it to David?

Further activity

Imagine you are David and you are being interviewed by the police as the only witness to this extraordinary happening. Write a script setting out the interview.

- Plan out a series of questions that the police would use.
- Do you think David would tell them the whole truth?
- Do you think the police would believe David?
- How do you think the interview would end?

8

Under the Ice

Very few people have actually seen a ghost. I have. But I wish I hadn't.

Rupert saw it long before I did, and I was the only person he ever told about it. I just wish he'd kept quiet, and then things might have turned out differently – at least I wouldn't have been there on that terrible day and I would never have seen what I did see. And I would never have known how unfair it was. There was no justice in it. None.

I have often thought I could have done something to stop it – but now I know that was impossible; I couldn't have done a thing. I'm only telling you this because I can't keep it to myself any longer.

I suppose you'd expect anybody who'd seen a ghost to tell everyone about it. Rupert was different. He kept things to himself. Quite a lot of people are like that, out in the flat fens. He had nobody much to talk to, so he got out of the habit, even with me, and I was always reckoned to be his best friend. He was a thin, gangly sort of boy, a bit taller than me, and he was tough in all sorts of ways you'd never guess just by looking at him.

I knew something was bothering him, but I didn't know what, although it had to be pretty important because one day, out of the blue, he asked me if I'd go home with him after school. It was a half holiday, in the middle of a bitter winter, and I didn't fancy cycling such a long way.

'It'll be dark before long,' I said, trying to make an excuse.

'That doesn't matter,' he said in a rush. 'My father will take us, and we can go skating. There's no danger, the ice is rock hard… So that'll be all right, will it?'

'Hold your hosses,' I said. This wasn't like Rupert at all, the quiet boy from far out of town. 'What am I going to do with my bike?' I wasn't going to leave that in the cycle shed all night, not with some of the characters I knew hanging about. 'And what about my tea – my mum'll be expecting me.'

'I'll give you some tea,' he said, just as if he owned the whole house, the bread and butter and everything. 'Give your mum a ring – and you can put your bike in the boot.' His father had a Volvo like a battle tank, so that was OK.

'Skates,' I said. 'I haven't got any.' My lovely brother in the sixth form nicked everything that belonged to me. 'William's screwed my skates on to his boots,' I told Rupert, 'so what's the use?'

'How big are your feet?' he said suddenly.

'Not as big as his.'

'Same size as me.' He plonked his foot down next to mine. 'You can have my old fen runners.'

'Gee,' I said. 'Thanks a million.'

He went red. 'Or you can have my Norwegians. I don't mind.'

'Don't worry about it, Rupe.' I was beginning to feel sorry for him; he seemed so eager for me to go with him that it would have been just like disappointing a little kid if I'd said no. So I said yes. You never do know what you're letting yourself in for.

He was in a fidget waiting for his father after school and he didn't calm down until we'd stowed the bike and were sitting side by side in the back seat. You could have told it was a farmer's car by the old fertiliser sacks in the boot, but even the back of his father's neck would have let you into the secret because it was brown and creased, and the trilby hat he wore was a mud colour through always being out in the sun and rain. I used to get on with his father quite well, chatting about this and that, but I hadn't seen him for some time, and now he was like Rupert – so quiet that after a while I began to feel as if he was some sort of servant in the front seat, just doing his job by driving us home. This made me so awkward that I kept silent, too.

Rupert practically ignored me. He sat back in his corner and gazed out of the window with his mind on something else while the heater blew warm air at us and I began to wish I was at home by the fire. If I'd had any sense I would have stopped feeling sorry for myself and would have remembered what it was that kept them so subdued. Everybody knew what had happened last summer, but that afternoon it just didn't come into my mind.

It had been freezing for a week so I was used to a nip in the air when I was cycling home, but when we got to where Rupert lived and stepped out of the car the cold was something else. In town it lay in chunks like massive ice cubes between the houses and you felt you could dodge some of it, but out here, where there were no streets and no street lights, the cold was a solid black mass that seemed to press even the birds to the ground.

'Don't know what there is to eat,' said Rupert's father. 'Bread and pull-it, I reckon.' I couldn't tell if he smiled because he turned his head away, but I guessed he didn't bother. 'The wife wasn't expecting anyone.'

Nice welcome, I thought, but I was polite. 'I don't mind, Mr Granger,' I said. 'I'm not very hungry.'

'That's all right, then,' and he left us, striding away over the crackling gravel to the farm outbuildings.

'I don't think I should've come,' I said, but Rupert was already taking me past the frozen bushes to the back door.

He went ahead of me, and the instant the door opened his mother gave a little cry and called out 'Who's there?' as if we were burglars. Even when Rupert told her it was just the two of us she kept peering over his shoulder to make sure exactly who was following him out of the shadows.

'It's only me,' I said.

'Oh,' she said, and some of the alarm went out of her eyes, but the worry remained. 'David Maxey. What are you doing here?'

This time even Rupert could tell I wasn't being given a very warm welcome, and he was embarrassed. 'He's hungry,' he said.

'But you never said you were bringing anyone.' She was quite bitchy with him. 'You never told me.'

I butted in. 'I'm sorry, Mrs Granger,' I said, and wished more strongly than ever to be somewhere else. 'It's Rupert's fault. He wants me to go skating.'

'Skating?' The idea seemed to confuse her.

'Mother.' Rupert went close to her. 'You know you don't like me to go skating on my own – so that's why I brought him. Two together are quite safe.'

She was looking from one to the other of us, and I said, 'If she cracks she bears, if she bends she breaks.' It was something they said about the ice in the fens, where everybody was a skater and knew about such things. 'It's very thick now, Mrs Granger, and it'll never bend an inch.'

She didn't answer. Instead, she turned to the dresser and took down plates to set a new place for me. 'I'm afraid there's not much,' she said.

I'd always liked Rupert's mother. She'd never seemed as if she belonged out here, miles from anywhere, with no neighbours. It was partly the way she dressed I suppose, as if she was ready to leave the farm behind at that instant and take us both up to town for a good time. But now there wasn't a trace of make-up on her face, and the shadows around her eyes were genuine.

'I'll get the skates,' said Rupert. 'They're in the garage.'

I didn't want him to leave me, but I made the best of it by trying to help his mother. There wasn't as much on the table as I was used to when I went there, and she apologised. 'I haven't been able to get out to the shops in this weather,' she said. It wasn't true; there hadn't been enough snow to make the roads dangerous, and I knew she had her own car.

'This is fine, Mrs Granger,' I said. 'I can hardly eat a thing.'

At any other time she would have seen through the lie and laughed; now she just turned towards me, her face full of anxiety, and said, 'Are you sure? Are you really sure?'

I'd always thought that, as mothers go, she was rather pretty, and I was so shocked at how pale and lined her face had become that I found I had no words, and I was very relieved when Rupert returned with the fen runners for me. The little skates, which were like the blades of table knives set in blocks of wood, were those he'd started with when he was younger. The boots were tight, but I managed to squeeze my feet into them.

Dusk was beginning to fall by the time we'd eaten and left the house. Mrs Granger stood at the door with her hands clenched in front of her as if she had to struggle not to reach out and hold us back.

'The ice is rock hard, Mrs Granger,' I said, making a new attempt to stop her worrying. 'We couldn't go through it even if we tried.'

'Don't,' she said, 'please don't say things like that.' She looked around the yard. 'Rupert, why don't you get your father to go with you?'

But Rupert was already walking away and his father, who had not joined us at tea, was nowhere to be seen.

I'd always known that the farmhouse was lonely, but I'd never realised just how isolated it really was until I caught up with Rupert on the road outside. In summer, green trees and bushes and tall grass crowded around the house and disguised its loneliness, but now the curtains of leaves had been stripped away, and the flat fields, the black furrows ridged with white, stretched away like the bare boards of an empty house.

'Cold,' I said, and the blades of the skates that swung in our hands rattled like chattering teeth.

The proper road petered out just beyond the farmhouse and became a track that only tractors could use. There were no hedges out here, only ditches with thin crusts of ice where

14

the water had seeped away beneath. I would have stopped to throw stones through the ice sheets except that Rupert was hurrying ahead, intent on getting somewhere – even though there seemed to be no place better than any other out here.

'It's getting dark early,' he said. 'It's all this cloud. You won't be able to see it soon.'

'See what?' I asked, but he had run on as if he didn't want to answer.

We came to a gate across the track and beyond it a low bank stretched away to left and right like the rampart of an ancient fort. On the other side lay the waterway, except that now it was an iceway, reaching in a dead straight line to the black horizon.

'When there's a moon,' said Rupert, 'you can skate out of sight.'

Our voices were so small in the vast space that I doubt if they reached the far bank of the wide channel, not that there was anybody in the whole of creation to hear us. An ice age had made the world a waste land, and we were alone in it.

'Where are you taking me?' I asked, because I'd guessed by now that he had something more than skating on his mind.

'Hurry up and get those runners on,' he said, and he had laced up his Norwegians and was crabbing down the bank almost before I'd started. I heard his long blades strike the ice as I still struggled with my laces. 'Wait for me,' I called, because he was already gliding out from the bank.

'Hurry up. It's getting dark.'

He was out in the middle of the channel when I reached the edge, caught the tip of one skate in a tussock of frozen grass and stumbled forward. I was sure I was going to get a wet foot in the seepage that is always at the margin, but my blades ran through the grass on solid ice. It was as hard as a marble floor from bank to bank. There was no risk of falling through; none at all – but Rupert was leading me on to a danger that was much worse.

We skated, sawing the air with our arms and feeling it bite back at our cheeks and noses, but he, riding high on blades twice the length of mine, easily outpaced me, and I was so far behind that there must have been a hundred metres of ice between us when I saw him circling, waiting for me to catch up.

I was a breathless plodder following a racehorse, and I had lost patience with him so I deliberately dawdled, bending low from time to time, merely letting myself slide slowly along. It must have been infuriating for him, but he gave no sign of it, and continued to cut his slow circles as I drifted closer.

'We don't need a moon,' I called. 'You can still see for miles.' The scatter of snow had made the banks white enough to catch all the thin light that came from the sky and we stood out like dark birds gliding low over frozen fields. But what food would birds find out here? What could they peck at? I was soon to find out.

'I'm flying!' I cried, and I leant forward and spread my arms wide. He had stopped and was waiting for me, and I wondered if I could reach him without pushing again, so I allowed myself to glide.

I was looking down, watching the little blades of the fen runners barely rocking as they skimmed forward, and I realised how smooth the ice was. It was a glassy pavement, polished, without cracks or blemishes, and it came as a shock to see that it was so clear I was actually looking through it. Even in this light I could see into the dark water below, where I knew the long weeds trailed in summer, and I gazed down into a giddy blackness.

My glide had been so successful that I was laughing as my skates came to rest almost at Rupert's feet, and I was just about to raise my head when I caught a glimpse of something beneath the ice. At first I thought it was a twist of weed, and I stooped to look closer. The shape became clear, and in that instant it reached inside me with a sick coldness that held me fixed to the spot. And then, horrified, not wanting to touch the ice anywhere near what I had seen, I eased myself backwards, still crouching, and stood up.

It was only then that I raised my eyes to Rupert.

There was a bridge behind him, in the distance. It was a single span where the track from the farm crossed the channel, and I remember it because it made a black shadow on a level with his shoulders and he seemed for an instant to have enormous arms that stretched from bank to bank. At that awful moment even he terrified me, and I was beginning to draw further back, when he spoke.

'So you can see it, too.' The words were like frost on his lips.

I nodded. I saw it clearly. There was a drowned man under the ice.

I could see the folds of his trousers and a shoe twisted at an awkward angle. The sleeves of his jacket were rigid, but his fingers seemed to lie at ease in the ice, resting, as plump and white as the flesh of a plucked chicken. His head was turned away from us, so all we saw was hair and one ear.

I said something, but I can't remember what. All I knew was that we had to go for help even if it was too late – we had to let someone know. That object locked beneath us had to be freed. Words came from me, but Rupert did nothing. He stood quite still.

'Look again,' he said.

I turned my eyes to the ice between us but I must have drifted too far back because now I could see nothing. I edged forward. The ice was black, and empty. I cast around, stooping to peer closer, but nothing showed itself.

'Where is it?' I said. The hideous thought came to my mind that a current still flowed under the ice and that the man was rolling slowly beneath our feet. 'Where is it now?' I was beginning to panic, taking timid steps on my skates away from the spot as if the ice were about to open and take me down to join the corpse in its frozen coffin. 'Where?' I said. 'Where?'

'It's still there.' His voice was so flat and calm it made me jerk my head up. 'It's my uncle,' he said.

He skated slowly forward. The extra height of his Norwegians made him tower over me, and once again I was afraid of him. His uncle! He had seen his uncle dead under the ice, and now he was gliding towards me without a sign of grief or even surprise on his face. I was backing clumsily away when he came level with me, and a thin smile appeared on his lips.

'You're not thinking of skating backwards all the way home, are you?' he said.

The fact that he could say something so ordinary, and smile as he spoke, jolted me out of my panic. I even managed to shrug. 'How can it be your uncle?' I began ... and then I remembered. It all came flooding back to me, and at the same instant I knew why his mother was so haggard and his father so silent. The tragedy that had slipped from my mind was still strong within them.

'Oh,' I said feebly, 'your uncle.'

And then my stomach turned over yet again, for his uncle had been dead many months, drowned out here in the fens.

'That was where it happened,' Rupert said. 'Last summer.'

I was ashamed of myself for having forgotten, and for a moment this blotted everything else from my mind. 'I'm sorry,' I said. 'I should have remembered.'

'I was there when he was found.' He began to move away. 'That's how I know who it is in the ice.'

So there really was a body there ... but he was talking nonsense to say it was his uncle. 'It can't be,' I said. 'It's just some old clothes.'

'With fingers?'

'Well, it's another body.' I didn't want to admit it. 'Someone else. We've got to tell somebody. We've got to.'

He said nothing. He moved away and I went with him. Our skates were silent and we drifted like ghosts through the bitter dusk. I twisted my head to look behind.

'There's nothing to see,' he said. 'Even if you go back you won't find it. It's gone.'

19

'How do you know?'

He turned a gaunt face towards me, and once again he smiled. 'Do you think I haven't tried?'

'But I saw it. If I can see it, so can somebody else. Have you tried to show anybody?'

Suddenly, as though we were racing, he lowered his head and stretched his legs in long, sweeping strokes that left me behind. I did not catch up with him until we reached the place where we had left our shoes. He was already crouching on the bank unlacing his boots. 'Too late to go any further,' he said. 'Too dark.'

We had just seen something impossible to explain, and that was all he had to say.

'It was a ghost,' I said, 'wasn't it?' And when that had no effect on him, I added, 'Or a shadow or something. Some sort of cracks and bubbles in the ice. The light might just catch them at times.' He remained silent, but I wasn't going to leave it there. 'You ought to tell somebody about it,' I said. 'Why not your mother?'

'She's got too much on her mind.' He concentrated on his laces for a while, and then, speaking so low I could hardly hear him, he said, 'She liked my uncle. She liked him a lot.'

'Well, you've got to speak to your father – you've got to tell him.'

'I can't.' He shook his head without looking up. 'I can't.' His fingers ceased fumbling with his laces but his head remained bowed, and after a while I saw his shoulders tremble and I realised he was crying.

We were side by side in the frozen grass and Rupert had

bent his head to his knees and was sobbing like a little child. I had never seen him in tears; and now that it had happened, I did not know what to do. I began unfastening my own skates, waiting until his sobbing subsided, trying to think of something to say, and failing. His grief was too deep for me to reach. Then, suddenly, he raised his head and was once again speaking clearly.

'He hated him,' he said. 'My father hated him. They used to be friends and then he hated him.'

'But they were brothers.'

'What difference does that make?' His voice was harsh. 'He liked my mother! My uncle liked my mother, didn't he? A lot. Too much. I heard him say so, didn't I?'

He spat the words at me so fiercely I had to face up to him. 'I don't know what you heard,' I said.

'I heard everything!' He sucked in his cheeks and glared at me as though I was the most detestable creature on earth. 'My father said he'd kill him if he didn't go away. Kill him!' He stooped forward suddenly and hauled off his skates. 'Now you can go home,' he said. 'Get lost!'

Neither of us said another word. I climbed the bank alone and got to his house ahead of him. I could see his mother and father through the kitchen window, but I didn't go in. I was in a hurry to get away from that place, so I found my bike and left.

The freeze got worse. Rupert and I saw each other at school and were still friends, but we never once mentioned what had happened. His outburst seemed to have shut the door on it, and there was a kind of haughtiness in him that made me see that he was so deeply ashamed of what he had told me he could never speak of it. I told myself that what I had seen in the ice was made by weeds frozen near the surface, and that it was Rupert's imagination, because of the terrible time he'd been through that had somehow forced us both to see what he'd seen last summer when they found his uncle.

Then one day the sun shone. The clouds, that for weeks had ground their way towards the horizon as slowly as a glacier, showed gaps of blue, and the sun began to put its fingers through the thin crust of snow on gardens and gutters. Even Rupert smiled and said, 'We shan't get much more skating this year, I reckon.'

'Too bad,' I replied, thinking that he wanted to shrug the whole business away for ever.

'So why don't you come over tomorrow before it's too late?' he asked.

He had taken me by surprise and I looked so sharply at him that he reddened and mumbled something, saying that there were bound to be other people around as it was a Saturday, so there was nothing to worry about. It was the nearest he'd come to mentioning what was on our minds, and I was a bit nettled that he thought I may have been afraid to go skating alone out there, so of course I said yes.

I even managed to get my skates from my brother, so I was properly equipped when I cycled out to see him. The sun was bright, but I had to push against a biting wind which kept the temperature so low that I knew the ice would still be in good

22

condition. And Rupert was right about other people being there. You could never say the ice was crowded because there was so much of it, but there were skaters wherever you looked, and their tiny black figures were dotted away into the distance. An occasional speed man came slicing by, one arm behind his back and the other swinging, and we decided we would join these long-distance skimmers.

Without either of us saying a word we set out towards the distant bridge and this meant we had to go over the spot where the shadows had frightened us so badly. We did not ignore it, but neither did we linger. We circled once, gazing down, and I was certain of the exact spot because the ice there was clear even though its surface was now criss-crossed by blade strokes. The sunlight would have shown any dead man beneath the ice, but there was nothing. There was only darkness below, and when I looked up and caught Rupert's eye he grinned sheepishly and skated off at speed as if to put it behind him once and for all.

We could hear the squeals of girls and the shouts of boys long before we reached the little groups that were strung out over the ice, but we skimmed by until we were far out in the fens. The sun, although now a blazing red, had shed the last of its heat for the day and was beginning to bury itself in the horizon before we thought of turning back. We stretched out on the frozen grass for a few minutes to rest our ankles.

'It's good out here,' said Rupert. He was panting and there was even some colour in his cheeks. 'I'm glad you could come today.'

We weren't in the habit of paying each other compliments, so I just mumbled that I, too, was enjoying myself. I expected the matter to end there, but Rupert had something on his mind; unfinished business.

'Sorry I was such an idiot last time,' he said.

'That's OK.' I didn't look at him.

'It's just that everything was getting on top of me – Mum and Dad not being very happy and all that. Things had just been getting worse and worse, ever since…'

He seemed to want me to say it for him.

'I know what you mean,' I said, but that wasn't good enough for him; he wanted it out in the open.

'Since my uncle drowned himself.' He spoke very clearly, forcing me to look at him. 'Drowned himself,' he repeated. 'I told you something stupid about my dad last time. It wasn't true.'

'I know it wasn't.' I had to agree with him. His father could never have done such a terrible thing as murder his brother, no matter what he might have said. 'You were feeling pretty bad,' I told Rupert. 'And we'd just seen that thing in the ice.'

'*Thought* we'd seen. It's not there now.'

'And it wasn't there then,' I insisted, backing him up. 'It was just imagination. By both of us.'

'Both of us.' He nodded. He was glad he had a friend, and to know that between us we'd scattered all the shadows from his mind. 'Right,' he said, 'I'll race you back.'

It was no race. He had done much more skating than me and his ankles were stronger, so from time to time he had to wait for me to catch up. We had gone further out into the fen

24

than I had realised and, with my slow progress, the sun had dipped below the horizon and had left only an afterglow before the bridge came in sight.

We were alone, the other skaters having long since climbed the banks and gone home, so when we came up to the bridge it was our voices alone that echoed beneath it.

'One at a time,' said Rupert. 'The thaw has made it wet under there.'

He went first. There was no suggestion of a crack as he went forward cautiously, but when I followed I could see that his weight had made a pulse of water spill from the edge, so I kept to the centre as he waited for me to come through.

I was concentrating so intensely on the ice beneath my skates that I almost ran into him and had to make a wide swerve to keep my balance. That was why I saw his father before he did. Mr Granger was at the top of the bank, looking down.

'Where have you been?' he called to Rupert. 'Your mother was worried.'

Rupert did not answer. He was leaning forward like a runner trying to get his breath, and I went up alongside him to taunt him. He did not even turn his head my way and I was stooping to look into his face when I saw that, although his mouth was open, he was not gasping for breath. He was in the grip of terror.

I did not wish to follow his gaze, but I was forced to turn my head and look down.

It was there. I saw the frozen shoe and trouser leg, the stiff folds of the jacket and the fingers cased in ice. Even the hair on the back of the twisted head was visible.

Neither Rupert nor I moved. We were locked to that dreadful place.

'What are you doing down there?' It was his father's voice from the bank. 'It's time to go home.'

I had my hand on Rupert's arm. I was beginning to pull him back, gently tugging at him, and my skates were making a faint rasping sound on the ice when it happened. The head began to turn. It was as though I had been scratching at the other side of a window pane and had aroused it. The head within the ice came round to face us. Yellow cheeks and an open mouth. And then the eyes, tight shut.

'What's happening?' Mr Granger's voice died and, as it did so, leaving the air empty of all sound, the eyelids lifted. A handspan of ice lay over them, but the eyelids slipped back like a flicker of moonlight, and a pair of dead eyes, grey and as pale as milk, stared up at us.

The cold air brushed the back of my neck as I jerked backwards, but Rupert did not stir. He remained where he was as the fingers came through the ice, and with them, the bulge of the head. It came up like a sleeper pushing back a sheet.

I heard Rupert's name shouted from the top of the bank, and his father came thudding and slithering towards him and snatched him away.

I had slid backwards and was beneath the bridge when the dead figure stood upright and came to collect them. Water ran from its sleeves and dripped from its pale, plump fingers, and its sodden shoes swished on the ice as it advanced.

Without realising it, I had backed even further away, out of the shelter of the bridge, so I was clear of what happened. I was a spectator ... as Rupert should have been. But he was with his father.

I saw them enter the shadow of the dark arch together, and I saw Rupert slip and fall full length. His father stooped for him, but never got a chance to lift his son upright. The dripping figure came moving towards them and, in the black shadow under the bridge, embraced them both.

The impact of Rupert's fall had been too much for the ice. There was a soft, rending crack and a sheet the size of a table up-ended itself and in an instant, without a sound, the huddle of figures had gone. I flung myself forward, but the ice had slid back into place. I kicked it, but it was wedged. I put my full weight on its edge, and still it did not budge. I knelt and hammered on it, but Rupert was with his father on the other side of that door, and I never saw him again.

Notes for Mayday!

Summary

This is a very short story. A dramatic situation unfolds very rapidly as problems develop during a flight in a passenger aircraft. At the beginning of the story everything seems to be routine and then, one after another, things begin to spiral out of control. As the aircraft hurtles out of control towards the ground, a helping hand intervenes.

What do you think?

This story shows that tension and suspense can be built up very quickly, and that some of the best stories around have a mysterious element. As you read, think about the following:

- Why does the writer include lots of technical details about aircraft and flying at the beginning of the story?
- What effect does the description of the moon have on the reader?
- How does the tension build up in the story?
- What do you think of the ending?

Questions

1. Is there a reason for Ian Sercombe to be frightened at the beginning of the story? Compare his feelings to those of the rest of the crew.

2. Explain what happened to Ian's friend, Mike Payne.

3. In spite of the emergency, a feeling of calm comes over the story – identify when and why that happens.

4. How does Ian regain control of the aircraft?

5. Do you think this is a ghost story? Give reasons for your answer.

Further activity

Imagine that you are one of the crew and you have to write a formal report of the incident for your superiors. Give a factual account of the incident. After you have written the report, you write an e-mail to your best friend describing the incident and explaining what happened. What differences are there between your two accounts?

Mayday!

Captain Ian Sercombe was frightened. He rested a broad forefinger on the control column of the Boeing 747 and eased back in his seat. Glancing out of the cabin windows at the sixty metres of his giant machine's wingspan he tried to calm himself with thoughts of its size and detail ... as high as a six storey building, over two hundred kilometres of wiring, four million parts, space for more than four hundred passengers ...

'Decent night, Skip.'

First Officer Les Bright's voice cut in on Ian's thoughts. The two men had completed the pre take-off check and were sitting on the flight deck. Outside a huge moon hung in the hot tropical night sky which pressed down on Singapore's Changi Airport.

Les Bright was talking to the control tower when Cabin Service Director Edwina Reeves came into the flight deck area.

'Two hundred and sixty passengers and thirteen cabin crew all safely on board, Captain. Cabin secure.'

'Thanks, Edwina,' replied Ian. 'We should be off very soon.'

Minutes later the huge aircraft began to roll away from its stand at the airport. The time was 8.04pm and the journey to Perth, Australia had begun.

Within an hour all was routine on the flight deck. The Jumbo was cruising at Flight Level 370, about seven miles above sea level. Speed was 510 knots and the course was 160° magnetic as the plane, under the automatic pilot, headed south over Indonesia.

'Weather ahead looks good,' commented First Officer Bright, nodding at the weather radar screen which promised three hundred miles of smooth flying ahead.

'Hmmm,' agreed Ian.

He had been studying the weather radar with unusual intensity – just as he had all the other complex instruments in the cabin. But the fear wouldn't go away. It wasn't nervousness … or apprehension … Ian Sercombe was frightened. He could only ever remember feeling like this once before, and that had been the dreadful day of the accident …

Ian and his lifelong friend Mike Payne had been crewing together on a flight back from New York. Leaving the airport in Ian's car, they were accelerating on the M25 when a tyre burst. In the crash which followed Ian had been unhurt, but Mike was killed instantly. Just before the tyre went Ian had felt this unreasoning fear. Afterwards he could never quite rid himself of guilt for Mike's death. He'd been blameless perhaps – he'd checked the tyres just a couple of days previously – but how could Mike know that? Once again he thought of Mike's bluff, smiling Irish face, grinning as always and clapping those gloved hands together. Always been a joke between them that – the only pilot who never flew without wearing fine kid gloves.

Ian's thoughts were brought back to the present as First Officer Bright made a routine position report.

'Jakarta Control, Moonlight Seven over Halim at 20.44.'

Then it started.

'Unusual activity on weather radar, Captain.'

'I see it, Les.'

'Just come up – doesn't look good.'

'Could be some turbulence in that. Switch on the "Fasten Seat Belts" sign.'

The two pilots tightened their own seat belts. Behind them in the crowded cabins, passengers grumbled as they had to interrupt their evening meal to fasten their seat belts. Smiling stewardesses assured them there was no problem.

'Engine failure – Four!'

The flight engineer's terse voice cut the flight deck silence.

'Fire action Four,' responded Ian simultaneously.

Together Les Bright and Engineer Officer Mary Chalmers shut off the fuel lever to Four and pulled the fire handle. There was no fire in the engine and Ian felt an easing of his tension.

No pilot likes an engine failure, but the giant Jumbo could manage well enough on the three that were left.

'Engine failure Two.'

Mary Chalmers' voice was more urgent this time, but as she and Les Bright moved to another emergency procedure she suddenly gasped breathlessly.

'One's gone … and Three!'

Seven miles high with two hundred and seventy-three people on board, the Boeing was now without power. Ian knew that the huge plane could only glide – and downwards.

'Mayday, Mayday, Mayday!' First Officer Bright's voice

barked into the emergency radio frequency. 'Moonlight Seven calling. Complete failure on all engines. Now descending through flight Level 360.'

Ian's hands and mind were now working with automatic speed. He again checked the fuel and electrical systems. Emergency restarting procedures failed to have any effect. Quickly he calculated their terrible position. The plane was dropping at about two hundred feet per minute … which meant that in twenty-three minutes time …

'You two,' said Ian quietly to the First Officer and Flight Engineer. 'I'm going to need all the help I can get later on, but there could be problems back there with the passengers now – especially as we're obviously going down. Go back – help out – and get back here as soon as you can.'

Bright and Mary Chalmers climbed out of their seats, slamming the door to the flight deck behind them as they went to try and reassure the terrified passengers.

Ian was now alone on the flight deck.

'Problems,' he muttered aloud. 'Crash landing in the sea so keep the wheels up, lights are going to fail because there's no generated power from the engines, standby power from the batteries won't last long …'

The closing of the flight deck door interrupted Ian's monologue.

'All right back there?' he asked, as the First Officer climbed back into his seat. He was just able to make out his fellow pilot's quick nod in the rapidly dimming light on the flight deck.

'It's too risky to try and get over those mountains now,' said Ian. 'What do you think?'

'Go for the sea,' was the reply, in a strangely muffled tone.

Ian's arms were aching from holding the lurching and buffeting aircraft, but he was surprised when the First Officer leaned over and laid a hand on his shoulder. It seemed to have both a calming and strengthening effect.

'I'll take her for a while.'

The giant plane continued to drop. At 14,000 feet the emergency oxygen masks had dropped from the roof for passengers' use. Now the rapidly dropping height was down to 13,000 feet.

'I'll save myself for the landing,' muttered Ian, watching his co-pilot in admiration. In the dim light the First Officer was a relaxed figure, almost caressing the jerking control column. His touch seemed to have calmed the aircraft too. Its descent seemed smoother, almost gentle even.

13,000.

12,000.

11,000.

'Ian.'

The captain was startled by the unexpected use of his Christian name by the First Officer.

'Volcanic dust and jet engines don't mix. I think we should make another re-light attempt on the engines now.'

Still feeling calm, even relaxed considering the terrible situation they were in, Ian began the engine restarting drill yet again.

'Switch on igniters ... open fuel valves ...'

As suddenly as it had failed, Engine Four sprang back into life.

'We've got a chance!' cried Ian.

'Go for the rest,' was the quiet reply.

Expertly, Ian's hands repeated the procedure. There was a lengthy pause then ... Bingo! Number Three fired ... then One ... and then Two.

'We'll make it after all,' sighed Ian, once again taking a firm grip of the controls.

'Les – get on to Jakarta Control and tell them what's happening ... Les ...'

To his astonishment, when Ian looked to his right only the gently swaying control column came into view. The First Officer had gone. It was then that the captain heard the crash of the axe breaking through the door to the flight deck.

Engineer Chalmers was the first one through the shattered door.

'Fantastic, Skipper, fantastic – how did you do it?'

'Incredible!'

This was Les Bright's voice.

'The flight deck door jammed and we've been stuck out there for five minutes wondering how on earth you were getting on – and now this! You're a marvel, Skipper.'

Ian glanced up at the animated face of his First Officer in the brightening light of the flight deck.

'But ...'

The rest of the words died on his lips. A feeling of inexplicable gratitude and calm swept over him. He remembered the confident, sure figure who had so recently sat in the co-pilot's seat. He now remembered too that just before the lights had reached their dimmest he had noticed that the hands holding the controls were wearing a pair of fine kid gloves.

'Get on to Jakarta,' Ian said quietly. 'Tell them we're coming in.'

Notes for Deserter

Summary
The Falkland Islands are a British province. In 1982 Argentinian soldiers invaded the islands but a task force of British soldiers fought them. This story is set at the end of the Falklands War and deals with the ideas of friends and enemies. A young boy is left on his own in the countryside while his parents transport wounded soldiers to hospital.

What do you think?
The description at the beginning of the story shows the devastation of war. By looking at the text try to work out what has happened between the English and Argentinian armies before this story starts. Think about the following:

- how the battleground is described
- the way Paco acts towards Eric when he first encounters him
- the way the story ends.

Questions
Back up your answers with quotations or references to the story.

1. What are Eric's feelings about the countryside in the Falklands? How does the writer show the strength of these feelings?
2. How does the writer create a false sense of security at the beginning of the story? Why does Eric leave the safety of his house?
3. How are Eric's surroundings in the cave described? What effect does this have on the story?
4. How does the relationship between Eric and Paco change during the story? How do they feel about each other at the end?
5. What do you think the attitude to war is in this story? Think of the significance of the title.

Further activity
Eric takes Paco back to the farmhouse. Write the script of his conversation with his parents.

- What is their attitude to Paco?
- How do they react to Eric's story?

Deserter

Eric gazed around him disbelievingly, his mouth dry and his heart pounding. The Falklands valley he had loved so much, with its unyielding grey rock, tussock grass and soft boggy ground, had been devastated, transformed into a man-made hell, a scrap-metal merchant's dream.

Bewildered geese fluttered over the debris of the battlefield, while cattle and sheep wandered aimlessly. Those were the lucky ones. Some were just carcasses, lying where they had been shot or blown apart by a mine.

Eric knew he shouldn't be here, that his parents had forbidden him to come anywhere near this dreadful place. But Buster, the Laker family's beloved old sheepdog, had gone missing.

Guessing he had probably been terrified by the sound of last night's battle, Eric was determined to look for him. The artillery fire, the blasting of anti-aircraft guns and the clattering of helicopters was still in his own ears. But maybe Buster was just dutifully trying to herd up the family's scattered sheep.

Eric wished his parents hadn't been asked to take away some of the Argentinian wounded. The ground was too soft for field ambulances and there weren't enough four-wheel drives, so Mr and Mrs Laker were heading for Port Stanley with the tractor and trailer, having told Eric to stay in the farmhouse. But neither of them had noticed Buster had gone and Eric knew he had to find him before he, too, stepped on a mine.

Increasingly afraid for the old sheepdog, Eric wove his way through the devastation, while the geese seemed to hang listlessly in the steel-grey morning sky. Then he began to run cautiously through the abandoned military equipment that covered the valley floor. Cannon shells, field dressings, machine guns, rifles, ammunition cases and spent bullets were everywhere amongst the craters, shell holes and shattered rock.

Eric shivered. He and his parents had sat through the night in an improvised bunker, listening to the Argentinian and British troops blowing each other apart. Now he could see the slit trenches of the Argentine positions and a number of rockets still lashed to long stout poles that protruded from the soft ground where sheep normally grazed. The sight was horrific.

A bitter wind blew a couple of helmets across the muddy ground towards him and freezing rain began to drum on the debris. Eric saw an open box of mortars, avoided a couple of camouflage nets, and then came across a boot. He didn't want to look any closer. Suppose it had part of a foot inside?

A couple of grubby white flags of surrender flapped in the beating wind and Eric hurried on, calling Buster, his voice thin and weak in the wilderness.

'The invasion's over,' his father had told him. 'There's been an Argentine surrender. You lock yourself in.'

But twelve-year-old Eric was determined to find Buster, whatever the dangers.

Eric knew that the Falkland Islands were among the bleakest and most desolate places on earth, but he had always loved his wilderness. He had lived on his parents' sheep farm all his life, except for an unhappy period when he had gone to boarding school in Buenos Aires on the Argentine mainland. Eric had hated the school – not because he was in Argentina, not because the work has hard and the lessons were in Spanish, but because he was desperately homesick for the rugged Falklands.

Eventually, Eric had become so unhappy in Buenos Aires that he had stopped eating and was flown home, to continue his education by radio on the Lakers' remote sheep farm.

On the edge of the battlefield, soaked and muddied almost beyond recognition, Eric noticed a Spanish Bible and was reminded of the young Argentine soldiers on the mountain last week. He and Buster had been moving the sheep along a twilit ridge when they had come across them. Some had been kneeling, while one lieutenant, wounded in the leg, had stood with a rosary in his hand. The soldiers had been lit by the flames of the gorse bushes they had set on fire to keep warm.

Eric had been as angry as any other Falklander when Argentina invaded the islands which had always been a British protectorate. The Argentines had announced they had come to reclaim territory which rightfully belonged to them, but the British had disagreed and their army had arrived to fight them off.

Eric had felt a sense of importance, of actually belonging to the United Kingdom, the far away country he had never seen. He wanted to be liberated and, judging by what Dad had said, he just had been. But at what cost? As he ran, he gazed around at the debris of war and wondered how many soldiers had died here.

Eric didn't care which side they were on; it was all such a waste. He had never hated the Argentines, never called them 'Argies', as some of the Falklanders and most of the British did. After all, he had been to school with them. He knew the Argentines. He didn't know the British.

'Buster!' Eric yelled into the raw bitterness of the rising wind and rain. 'Where are you, Buster?' Suppose the dog was dead? Eric's eyes began to sting with tears.

He gazed down at the cove, the spume rising as the waves tore at the black rock. Terns wheeled over the tumult, but he could just make out the sound of barking above their plaintive cries.

Then, to his joy, he saw Buster down on the pebbles of Sea Wrack cove, running in and out of a cave entrance, his bark becoming an angry howl.

'I'm coming, boy,' he yelled into the darting wind. 'I'm coming, Buster.' But he knew there was no chance of the old sheepdog hearing or even seeing him, as mist rolled up out of the ferocious sea. Without even thinking about the mines, Eric began to run as hard as he could, thankful that he was wearing heavy boots, jeans and a thick anorak.

He arrived on the beach in a flurry of mud and rain, still calling Buster's name. But the dog seemed to have retreated into the cave mouth.

What was the matter with him? Eric wondered, his relief draining away. Was there a sheep in there or had Buster been driven mad by the battle – just as some men must be? He could hear him barking faintly and paused. The caves were known as the Labyrinth, and they stretched for miles under the cliff. It would be all too easy to get lost in them. 'Folks have gone in and never come out,' his dad had warned him repeatedly.

What was he going to do? Eric called Buster over and over again, but his barking only seemed to get fainter.

Eric plunged into the darkness of the caves, listening intently for the sound of Buster's barking. Trying to remember the way, he kept reciting to himself, 'Left ... left ... left ... right ... left.' Soon he became confused. Hadn't it really been left, right, left? Or wasn't it left and then right?

Panic swept him and Eric found himself sweating, feverish, but determined to continue.

Soon the barking became much louder and, within seconds, illuminated by wan torchlight, Buster appeared, leaping up at something that was lying on a ledge.

Buster was still barking furiously.

Suddenly the beam shone directly into Eric's eyes, dazzling him. Someone was there. Someone different, alien. Terrified, he saw huge eyes that looked as if they were on stalks. The scream began in his throat and stuck there, vibrating inside him.

Then Eric realised what he was looking at and felt an utter fool. The man was wearing PNGs – passive night goggles – which were designed to intensify night images and were worn by British and Argentine soldiers alike.

The figure moved slightly, huddling away from Buster's still relentless barking, and Eric caught a glimpse of a light machine gun and the Argentine insignia on the torn and muddied combat jacket.

Trying not to panic, he placed a restraining hand on Buster's neck, reassuringly rubbing his fur, trying to calm him down but not succeeding. What was he going to do? Should he turn and run?

The soldier struggled to an upright position, putting the torch down on the rock and holding his machine gun in both hands.

'Water,' came the hoarse voice.

'I haven't got any. Are you hurt?'

The soldier didn't reply. Then, to his horror, Eric heard a click.

Had he taken off the safety catch on the machine gun? Was he going to kill them both? Then a sudden thought occurred to him. Why hadn't he shot Buster already?

Eric struggled to remember at least some of the Spanish he had learnt at the school in Buenos Aires, but the chill inside him had made his mind go blank. Eventually he managed, '*Te lastimaste?*' He repeated the phrase in English. 'Are you hurt?'

There was a long silence.

Then the hoarse voice replied, 'Yes.'

'*Soy un amigo,*' stuttered Eric. 'I'm a friend.' Well, he was hardly that but never mind, as long as he could persuade the soldier not to kill him. He felt a pounding in his temples, and a roaring in his ears.

Buster was growling softly now, as if he, too, knew of the terrible danger they were both in.

'Water,' repeated the soldier.

'I'll get some,' said Eric, backing off. 'I shan't be long.' Could this be his chance of escape?

The Argentine soldier dragged off his goggles. 'No,' he rasped. 'Don't move.'

Does he know the war's over? Eric wondered. Should he tell him? He decided to take the risk. 'Your army has surrendered.'

He felt the soldier's eyes on him.

'The Argentines have surrendered. The war's over.'

There was another long silence. Then the soldier muttered something and gave a grunt of pain.

Eric heard the click of a trigger. He shut his eyes and waited for the bullet to cut him down.

The soldier pulled the trigger again and Eric wondered if he had already been hit. He couldn't feel anything but perhaps he was already dying. He gasped for air.

There was a dry laugh and Eric opened his eyes. Immediately the rocky sides of the tunnel closed in on him and he staggered. The sense of relief was overwhelming and gradually the faintness passed. The soldier had been bluffing.

Or had he? He was now pointing the machine gun at Buster and Eric felt sick. 'Please don't,' he whispered, sure the soldier's finger was on the trigger now, that he was actually going to fire. 'Please,' he repeated as Buster growled.

Then he heard the sound of sobbing.

Eric gazed at his tormentor in bewilderment. The crying was desolate but also childish, and he knew the game was over.

'Empty,' the soldier muttered. He threw the gun down on the floor with a dull clatter but grabbed the torch.

'What's the matter?' Eric asked, but the sobbing continued

and he was reminded of how he had cried so bitterly on his own in Buenos Aires for love of the Falklands. Was the soldier doing the same for Argentina?

'Give me the torch,' suggested Eric hesitantly. 'Buster and I can guide you out.'

The soldier shook his head, trying to stifle his sobs, and on impulse Eric lunged forward, knowing how stupid he was being but somehow unable to stop himself. He had to get back in charge again. This was *his* island. He didn't want interlopers, whether they were Argentine or British.

Eric felt a kick in the stomach and, surprised at the softness of the impact, he nevertheless lost his balance and fell back on to the hard rock.

He struggled to his feet again, grabbing Buster's collar as the old sheepdog began to bark furiously. Then he saw the stinking bundle of rags wrapped around the soldier's foot.

'You *are* hurt.' He suddenly realised that the Argentine soldier had contracted trench foot, a condition he had already seen in British soldiers, caused by spending endless days and nights on the soggy soil. Continuously wet and sore, his foot had eventually gone rotten. Eric shuddered.

Then he saw that the young soldier had dropped the torch and it was lying on the rocky floor, the beam still shining. They both rushed for it at the same time, but Eric got there first and ran back up the tunnel, Buster behind him, expecting pursuit but hearing none. He stopped, waiting.

On impulse, Eric returned, shining the torch directly on the soldier's face. He was young, probably no more than eighteen, with a pale, oval face, short dark hair and a growth of beard.

Buster resumed his growling as Eric asked, 'What's your name?'

'Paco.'

'*Soy un amigo,*' he repeated, wondering what he was going to do next. 'Eric.'

Paco shrugged.

'You come home with me. Have food and drink.' Eric moved a little nearer and flashed the torch into the soldier's frightened eyes.

'They shoot.'

'I told you. It's all over. You'll be a prisoner of war.'

'*Argentines* shoot me. I run.'

So you're a deserter, thought Eric. You think you'll be shot by your own people. He could sense Paco's fear and shame and wondered fleetingly what he would have done if he had been in his place.

For a moment Eric felt a surge of contempt. Running away – leaving his comrades – it was a dreadful thing to do. But he couldn't help feeling moved by Paco's plight. '*Soy un amigo,*' he repeated. 'I'm your friend. I'll help you.' Eric paused. 'I mean – you can't stay down here for ever. You'll die.'

Slowly Paco got to his feet. 'I come,' he said.

Flustered, unsure of himself, Eric began to walk into the darkness, the torch seeming weaker now.

A few minutes later, he knew that he was lost in the Labyrinth. He was sure he had taken a number of wrong turnings.

Paco was groaning behind him, and every so often he gave a little yelp of pain. Far from finding the way, Buster refused to go in front at all, determinedly bringing up the rear as if to protect them from a surprise attack.

'*Estamos perdidos*?' asked Paco softly, and Eric stopped and turned round.

'Yes,' he said woodenly. 'We're lost.'

'Light.'

Eric looked down at the torch to see that its beam was definitely weakening.

Paco shook his head impatiently. 'Light!' he repeated, but this time he was pointing back the way they had come. 'I *see* light,' Paco explained, searching for words.

Eric stared at him blankly.

'Give.' He gestured urgently at the torch.

Eric paused. Suppose Paco ran away and left him and Buster alone in the dark. Then he realised that he wouldn't get very far with his trench foot.

Now it was Eric and Buster's turn to follow. Paco took them back the way they had come, flashing the still-weakening torch, successfully remembering the route until they eventually arrived in a large cave. Dull grey light lit the walls and Eric's heart raced.

Above them was a tall chimney in the rock with a small patch of sky at the very top. The first part of the climb looked easy, with ledges as well as nooks and crannies for hands and feet, but further up the chimney the rock was sheer.

'We'll try the tunnels again,' said Eric hopelessly. He felt completely incapable of tackling such a climb.

Paco, however, was still gazing up the shaft, as if he had

not heard him or, more likely, didn't understand. 'We climb,' he said.

'What about Buster?'

'Stay.'

'You'll have to go alone.' Eric was adamant. Buster looked up at him and whined.

Paco took an ammunition belt from around his shoulders and gestured that he wanted to tie Buster to an outcrop of rock.

'No,' said Eric. 'I'll stay with him.' Then he realised he still couldn't trust Paco. Suppose he did get up the chimney, even with his foot, and abandoned them? He and Buster might never be discovered.

'Give me that belt. I'll do it.'

Buster was eventually secured and Eric gazed up at the chimney doubtfully.

'OK?' asked Paco impatiently.

'Yes.' Eric noticed that the young Argentine seemed much calmer now, as if he was living for the moment, wiping out the future.

As they began to climb, Eric could see that Paco was in considerable pain but this didn't slow him up. Uneasily he realised that their positions had been reversed. Paco was in charge now.

They clambered on, breathing heavily, bracing themselves against the rock wall as it narrowed. Buster barked below, straining at his leash, and then began to howl. Eric tried to comfort himself with the thought that his father knew the

Labyrinth in great detail and would soon be able to rescue the old sheepdog, but it was terrible to hear him in such distress.

Eric didn't dare look down at the drop below. If he did that, if he thought too much about Buster's despair, he knew that he would fall. Nevertheless, his whole body began to shake.

Pausing to catch his breath, Eric saw that Paco had reached the sheer side of the chimney. The Argentine hesitated for a second and then, with a series of painful gasps, hauled himself up the rock face, relying on the strength in his wrists.

With a renewed feeling of dread, Eric realised that he was neither tall enough nor strong enough to do the same. He would crash down into the abyss, smashing himself to pieces in front of Buster.

'It's no good,' he shouted up to Paco. 'I can't do it.'

'Come.'

Clinging to the rock Eric gazed up to see that Paco was lying on a ledge, gripping the rock behind him with his legs, the sweat trickling into his eyes, one long arm extended.

'Come,' he said firmly.

'I can't reach,' yelled Eric.

He knew that he had to try. If he climbed slightly higher, got a strong foothold and pushed himself up, maybe Paco *could* grap him. But wasn't he too heavy? Would he pull Paco off? Then they would both tumble into the abyss.

Eric clambered up a little further and, balancing precariously, stretched up, made fleeting contact with Paco's hand and then clutched at the rock again, somehow steadying himself, sure that he was going to fall.

Buster's howling became louder.

'Don't let me go,' he whispered and then looked up into Paco's pale face. 'Please don't let me go.' Then, with a tremendous effort of will, Eric stood on his toes and stretched up again.

This time they made firmer contact and, although there was a dreadful moment when Eric thought his hand was slipping, Paco's grip on his wrist tightened. He was dragged up, bumping painfully against the rock, the roaring back in his ears.

For a moment Eric had the terrifying sensation of flying as his foot left the crevice. Then he suddenly found his chest scraping the ledge, which was much broader than he had imagined, despite the fact that Paco was taking up a good part of it.

Eric was still in his grip, being pulled along the rock, his legs dangling and then pumping furiously as he tried to get a hold.

He was on his own now, inching himself up, the exhilaration soaring, blood at his fingertips as he scrabbled at the rock.

At last they lay side by side on the ledge, gasping for breath.

The rest of the climb up towards the hard grey patch of sky was easy, despite the fact that it was made to the accompaniment of Buster's hoarse but still frantic barking.

Finally, Eric followed Paco out on to the tussock grass at the top of the cliff, looking down on the valley of death.

The freezing rain had lessened and mist was blowing in from the sea.

'Let's go home,' said Eric, struggling to his feet. 'My father will fetch Buster.'

But Paco didn't move, and Eric could see that his eyes were glazed with fear.

'You'll be a British prisoner of war.' Eric tried to reassure him. 'Come on. It's my turn to help you.'

He would tell his parents that the Argentine deserter had saved his life and they would pass the information on to the British army. But that was all he could do for him. That was all he could ever do.

Eric began to run down the cliff path with Paco close behind.

Notes for Gifts from the Sea

Summary

The Second World War is the historical setting for this story. After a bad bombing raid, Brian is sent to stay with his grandparents on the north-east coast of England. His favourite hobby is collecting souvenirs from the air raids and along the coast; but a discovery he makes while searching the beach changes his attitude to the war forever.

What do you think?

The description at the beginning of the story is very dramatic, as the effects of an air raid are felt by Brian and his parents. One theme of the story is Brian's changing attitude to war: he is excited by the idea of staying with his grandparents and later in the story by collecting his souvenirs. Other people in the story are affected by the war in different ways. As you read the story, think about the following:

- the effects of the war on Brian, his mum and dad, and his gran and granda
- how Brian shows that in some ways he is quite young and in other ways he is growing up
- why the story ends so suddenly.

Questions

Choose words or phrases from the story to back up your answers.

1. Explain why the first three paragraphs grab your attention.

2. What does Brian see from the train on his journey to his grandparents?

3. How has Castle Cliff changed?

4. How are the cod's heads described and why are they important later in the story?

5. How is Brian's character shown at the end of the story?

6. What do you think the writer's attitude to war is?

Further activity

Imagine that Brian writes a letter to his parents to tell them what he has been doing while he has been staying with his grandparents.

- Check how to set out an informal letter.
- Make a list of the details that you think Brian will tell his parents.
- Does he tell them about the 'mermaid'?

Gifts from the Sea

The next bomb was the closest yet. Its slow, descending screech got louder and louder and louder.

Brian began to count under his breath. If you were still counting when you reached ten, you knew it hadn't blown you to pieces. He stared at the curving white wall of the shelter, the candle flickering in its saucer. The last things he might ever see on this earth ...

Seven, eight, nine ... the bunk he was lying on kicked like a horse. The candle fell over and rolled round the saucer, still burning, and starting to drip wax on to the little table. From the top bunk, his mother reached with a nearly steady hand and set it upright again. They listened to the sound of falling bricks as a house collapsed, the rain of wood and broken slates pattering down on the road and thudding on to the earth on top of their shelter.

'Some poor bugger's gotten it,' said Mam.

After the all-clear had gone, they climbed out wearily into the dawn and saw which poor bugger had gotten it. Number ten was just a pile of bricks. Eight and twelve had lost their windows and half the slates off their roofs. The road was littered. A big black dog was running around in circles, barking at everything and everybody. An ambulance was just disappearing round the corner of the road, and a crowd of people were breaking up, where number ten had been. Dad came across, filthy in his warden's uniform. Mam stared at his face silently, biting her lip.

'It's all right, hinny.' He grinned, teeth very white in his black face. 'They were in the shelter. We got them out. They're not hurt. But she cried when she saw what was left of her house.'

'She kept it like a little palace,' said Mam. 'She was that proud of it.'

Dad looked up at the sky, the way the German bombers had gone.

'Aye, well,' he said, 'the RAF lads got one of the buggers.'

They trailed round to the back door of their house. The kitchen seemed just as they'd left it; only a little jug with roses on it had fallen on the floor and broken into a hundred fragments.

'That was a wedding present,' said Mam. 'Your Auntie Florrie gave us that.' She bent down wearily and began picking up the pieces.

But it was when they opened the front-room door that they gasped. The windows were still whole, and the curtains intact. But everything else was just heaps of whiteness, as if there'd been a snowstorm.

'Ceiling's down,' said Dad. Brian stared up at where the ceiling had been. Just an interesting pattern of inch-wide laths, nailed to the joists. Dad ran upstairs and shouted that the bedroom ceilings were down too.

'Eeh, what a mess,' said Mam. 'How we ever going to get this straight?' Brian could tell she was on the verge of tears. 'Me best room. Where can I put the vicar now, if he calls ...'

'Just thank God you've still got a house to clean, hinny,' said Dad gently. 'But,' he added, looking at Brian, '*you'd* better go and stay at your gran's, till we get this lot cleared up.'

An hour later, still unwashed, still without breakfast, Brian was on the little electric train down to the coast. He had Mam's real leather attaché-case on the seat beside him, with a change of underpants, pyjamas, a hot-water bottle and his five best Dinkie toys. He felt empty and peculiar, but excited. An adventure; you couldn't say he was running away like those evacuee kids. Gran, at the coast, was nearer the Jerry bombers than home. It was more like a holiday; no school for a week. And even more like a holiday because he was setting out before most kids were up. The train was full of men going to work in the shipyards. Blackened overalls and the jackets of old pinstripe suits; greasy caps pulled down over their eyes as they dozed. Everybody grabbed a nap when they could these days. But they all looked like his dad, so he felt quite safe with them.

He turned and looked out of the window, down at the river far below. Greasy old river, with brilliant swirls of oil on it. Packed with ships, docked three-deep on each bank. Big tankers; the rusty grey shapes of destroyers and corvettes. Already some welders were at work, sending down showers of brilliant electric-blue sparks, like fireworks in the dull grey morning.

Britain can make it, thought Brian. Britain can take it. He often heard Mr Churchill talking inside his head, especially when he felt tired or fed up. It helped.

The man beside him spoke to the man opposite. 'Aah see Gateshead's playin' Manchester City on Saturday.'

'Andy Dudgeon'll hold them.'

'City's good ...'

'Andy'll still hold them.'

Brian was last to get out. At Tynemouth. He walked down empty Front Street, sniffing the smell of the sea that came to greet him. *Just* like being on holiday. A Co-op cart was delivering milk. Brian felt so good and grown up, he almost stopped and told the milkman all about being bombed. But only a kid would've done that, so he only said good-morning.

Gran gave him a good breakfast. She cut her toast much thicker than Mam, and always burnt the edges in an interesting way because she toasted it with a fork on the open fire. It tasted strongly of soot, but there was a huge lump of butter in the dish that made up for it. He didn't ask where the butter had come from; he'd just be told that Granda knew a feller who worked down the docks.

After breakfast he helped Granda hoist the Union Jack on the wireless-mast in front of the row of coastguard cottages on the cliff. An act of defiance against Hitler. Granda ran it up the pole, broke out the tightly wrapped bundle with a vigorous tug on the rope. The flag fluttered bravely in the wind. Granda said 'God save the King' and they both saluted the flag. Then Granda said 'God help the workers', but that was just a joke. They always did it the same, when he stayed with Granda. Then Granda went to work, and Gran got out the poss-tub and the poss-stick, it being Monday morning, and started thumping the washing in the water as if Fatty Goering was somewhere down there in a midget submarine.

Washing-day was no time to be in the house. Wet washing hung in front of the fire, steam billowed, the windows misted up and even your hands felt damp. Brian got out, followed by a yell that twelve o'clock was dinner-time.

Everything was still terribly *early*. Brian felt hopelessly ahead of himself. Still, he had plenty of *plans*. First he called at the school, to stand grandly outside the railings and watch the local kids being marched in, and feel *free* himself. Then he went on to tour the defences; the sandbagged anti-aircraft pom-poms on the sea-front. He spent a long time hovering from foot to foot, enjoying the guns' shining, oily evilness, till a grumpy sentry asked him why he wasn't in school.

Then he headed down the pier. The pier was like a road, running half a mile out into the grey of the sea. It was like walking on the water. It was like walking into the wide blue yonder, like the song of the American Army Air Corps. It was like playing dare with the Nazis, across the sea in Norway. It was even better when waves were breaking over the granite wall, as they were today. You tiptoed along, listening for the sound of the next wave, and if you were lucky you just managed to duck down behind the wall before the wave broke, and stayed dry. Otherwise you got soaked to the skin, all down your front.

He dodged successfully all the way, feeling more and more omnipotent. At the far end he stood in the shelter of the enormous lighthouse and watched an armed trawler put to sea. It came speeding up the smooth water of the estuary, and then pitched like a bucking bronco as it was hit by the first sea wave. The wind blew its sooty smell right up to him, with the smell of grilling kippers from the galley chimney. Soot, salt, wind, spray and kippers blew around his head, so that he shouted out loud for joy, and waved to the men on the deck; and one of them waved back.

And then he suddenly felt lonely, out there so close to Hitler. Getting back to land was harder and scarier. The waves might creep up behind your back; so might a German bomber. They'd machine-gunned the lighthouse before now; they would machine-gun anything that moved, and most things that didn't. He took much longer getting back to shore, running sideways like a crab, looking back over his shoulder for waves and Germans.

At the end of the pier he met a dog, on the loose like himself. A big Alsatian, all wet and spiky-haired from swimming in the river, and thirsting for mischief. It shook itself all over him, then put its paws on his shoulders and licked his face all over with a long, smooth, pinky-purple tongue.

Then it stood by the steps down to the rocks and barked encouragingly. Brian stood doubtful. It was good fun going round the tumbled rocks at the base of the Castle Cliff, but dicey. The cliff was brown and flaky and crumbling; there'd been falls of rock. When his dad was a boy it had been called Queen Victoria's Head because, seen sideways, it had looked just like the profile of the old Queen on a coin: nose, chin, bust, everything. Then the cliff had fallen and the Queen was gone, and now the cliff looked like nothing at all.

The boulders at the foot were huge and green with seaweed, with narrow cracks in between, where you could trap and break your ankle. And if you trapped your ankle or broke it, and you were alone except for a dog that didn't know you, you would just have to lie there till the tide came in and drowned you and swept your body out to sea. Nobody else walked round Castle Cliff rocks on a weekday ...

The dog barked, insisting. Brian looked at the line of damp on the rocks, and decided the tide was still going out.

He followed the dog out on to the rocks, waving his arms wildly as he leapt from boulder to boulder, and his hobnailed boots slithered on the green weed and only came to a crunching stop in the nick of time, as they met a patch of white barnacles.

But almost immediately he was glad he'd come. He began to find things brought in by the tide. First a glass fishing-float, caught in a veil of black, tarry net. He scrabbled aside the net; underneath, the float was thick, dark green glass, half the size of a football. He dropped it inside his shirt, where it lay cool and damp against his belt, because he had to have both hands free for the rocks. Mam would like the glass float for her mantelpiece; it would help make up for the damage the Nazis had done to her house.

Then there was a funny dark piece of wood, about as big as an owl. At some time it had had a bolt driven through it, for there was a dark round hole, like an eye, at one end. It had been burnt too. It had ridged feathers of damp, blue-black, shiny charcoal. Brian looked out to sea, remembering ships bombed and burnt and sunk by the Nazi bombers, within sight of the shore ...

But the sea, and the grinding rocks, had worn the lump of

wood into the shape of folded wings and a tail, so that when he held it out upright in his hand, it *did* look like a bird, with a round dark eye each side of its head. The dog thought it looked like a bird too. It ran up, barking frantically, and neatly snatched the bird from his hand with one slashing grab. Then it discovered it was only wet wood and let it drop. It barked at it some more, then looked at Brian, head on one side, baffled.

He picked it up and held it out at arm's length again, waggling it to make it look alive. And again the dog thought it was a bird, and leapt and grabbed. Then dropped it, shaking its head vigorously, to get the sharp taste of salt out of its mouth.

He threw it for the dog, as far towards the sea as he could. It hit a boulder and leapt in the air with a hollow clonk. On the rebound, the dog caught it and slithered wildly down a sloping rock, ending up with a splash in a deep rock-pool. It brought the piece of wood back to him, and shook itself all over him, soaking him anew.

The fourth time he threw it, it clonked down a crack in the rocks and vanished out of sight. The dog tried to get down after it, but couldn't, and stood barking instead. Brian was suddenly sad; he would have liked to have taken it home and given it to his dad. His dad might have set it on a base and varnished it and put it on the mantelpiece. His dad liked things like that. As he stood, he heard the cautious voice of his dad inside his head telling him to be careful, or he'd be a long time dead. It made him check on the state of the tide, but he was sure it was still going out.

But he explored more cautiously after that. Found evil-smelling cod's heads from the fish-gutting, hollow-eyed like skulls, with teeth sharp and brown as a mummified alligator. He sniffed at the stink of rotting flesh, was nearly sick, and sniffed more gently a second time, till finally he could stand the smell without being sick. It was part of toughening yourself up for the War Effort ...

And then he found the patch of limpets, clinging to a rock. He hovered again. Limpets were his great temptation. They clung to the rocks so hard, you might have thought them stuck there for ever with glue. But he'd found out long ago they weren't. Under the shallow cone of the ribbed shell was a sort of snail, which clung to the rock with a great big sucker-foot. If the limpet heard or felt you coming, it put on maximum suction and you'd never get it off the rock. But if you crept up quietly, you could get the blade of your knife under it before it knew you were there, and you could flick it off upside down into the palm of your hand.

And there it was, all pale soft folds, gently writhing in its bed of liquid, all beautiful with its two eyes coming out on stalks, like snails' eyes ... It somehow gave him a squishy feeling, like the photos of semi-nude girls at the Windmill Theatre in London, which he snitched out of *Picture Post* after his parents had read it, and which he hid in an old tobacco-tin of his father's, under a pile of his own *War Illustrateds*.

He took his fill, till the feeling wore off, and then he carefully chose a smooth wet patch of rock and put the limpet back on it, right way up. He tested it; the limpet had resumed its grip on the rock, but only feebly. When the tide came back in, the waves might knock it off, and whirl it round and smash it … He felt somehow terribly, terribly guilty and wished he hadn't done it. But he could never resist, till afterwards.

The dog barked impatiently, summoning him on, not understanding why he was wasting the wonderful morning. He scrambled on after it, trying to stop worrying about the limpet.

They came round Castle Cliff at last, safe into King Edward's bay. Little, snug, a sun-trap his dad had called it, when they came down for the day before the war. Chock-full of bathers then, deck-chairs, ice-cream kiosks and places where you could get a tray of tea for a shilling, and a shilling back on the crockery afterwards.

Not now. Totally empty.

And divided into two halves by the wire; huge rolls of barbed wire, stretching like serpents from cliff to cliff. Inland of the wire, the beach was dead mucky, full of footmarks, dropped fag-ends, rusting, broken bits of buckets and spades. People still came here for a smell of the briny, even in wartime. Holidays-at-home … the government organised it … fat girls in their pre-war frocks, dancing with each other in the open air on the Prom, to the music of the local army band in khaki uniform; pretending they were having a hell of a good time, and hoping one of the band would pick them up afterwards …

Seawards of the wire, the beach was clean, smooth, pure, washed spotless by the outgoing tide. Sometimes the waves, at the highest tides, passed through the wire. Nothing else did. For there were notices with a skull and crossbones, warning of the minefields buried under the sand to kill the invading Jerries, or at least blow their legs off.

Unfortunately, the dog could not read. It went straight up to the wire and began to wriggle through, waggling its hips like a girl trying to catch a soldier's eye. Brian shouted at the dog, leaping up and down, frantic. Feeling responsible, feeling he'd brought it here. Forgetting *it* had brought *him*.

The dog took no notice. It finished its wriggling and leapt gaily on to the clean, wet, flat sand. It became sort of drunk with space and wetness and flatness, tearing round in ever-increasing circles, cornering so sharply its feet slid and it nearly fell on its side. Brian waited terrified for the small savage flash and explosion, braced to see large, furry, bloody bits of dog fly through the air, as if they were legs of pork in a butcher's shop before the war.

But nothing happened. The dog changed its tactics and began dive-bombing bits of wreckage that were strewn about, leaping high in the air, and coming down hard with all four feet together. Throwing things up in the air and catching them.

Why didn't the mines go off? That dog was as heavy as a grown man ... Then Brian looked at the sand under the wire. There were all sizes of dog-tracks running through it. The dogs of the town had obviously found out something the humans didn't know.

There were no mines. The army couldn't afford them. All they could afford were notices warning of mines. Then the people who read them would think they could sleep safe in their beds at night, thinking the mines were protecting them from the Germans.

Fakes. Like the fake wooden anti-aircraft guns that Tommy Smeaton had found up the coast towards Blyth, guarded by a single sentry against the English kids who might wreck them. Fakes, like the airfields full of plywood Spitfires that kids played in round the Firth of Forth ...

Brian didn't know whether to laugh or cry.

Then he followed the dog through the wire. Ran round in circles with it, teasing it with a long lump of seaweed. Jumped up and down expecting, still, with a strange half-thrill that there would be a bang under his feet at any moment, and he would go sailing through the air ...

No bangs. He sat down breathless, and all that happened was that the damp sand soaked through the seat of his shorts.

When he got his breath back, he began to explore along the tide-line. Oh, glory, what a haul! A sodden sheepskin boot with a zip down the front, obviously discarded by a pilot who'd had to ditch in the sea. And it was a size seven, and the seven had a strange crossbar on it, which meant it was continental. A German pilot's boot!

Then he found a dull brown tin that clearly said it contained ship's biscuits. Iron rations, floated from the lifeboat of some sunken ship! British, so not poisoned, like people said German things were. He'd take them home to Mam.

A cork life-jacket, good as new. Oh, glory, what a place for war souvenirs, and not a kid in the whole town must know about it! A near-new shaving-brush for Dad ... German or

British, it didn't matter. Dad's old one was pre-war, and nearly worn down to a stump.

His shirt-front began to bulge like a lady who was having a baby. Sea-water ran down under his belt, down the front of his shorts, but he didn't care. A brier pipe, an aluminium pan without a dent, a good broom-head, a lovely silver-backed mirror. He had his pockets stuffed, his hands full, things tucked under both armpits so he could hardly walk. In the end he had to make dumps of useful stuff, every few yards above the tide-line. He couldn't carry them all home at once; he must hide some, bury some in the dry sand and come back for it later.

The last find took his breath away. A violin in its case. The strings had gone slack; no sound came when he twanged them, but surely it must be worth a bob or two? Dad would know.

He moved on into sudden shadow. He looked up, and saw that he was nearly at the foot of the far cliff. Where the Mermaid's Cave was.

Nobody called it the Mermaid's Cave but him. He had found it in the last year of peace. There was nothing in it but a long floor of wet, glistening pebbles, full of the smell of the sea. But each pebble glowed wonderfully in the blue-lit gloom. It was a miraculous place; the kind of place you might expect to find a mermaid … if anywhere on earth.

Not that, at thirteen, he believed in mermaids any more. Only in soppy poems they taught you at junior school. 'The Forsaken Merman.' Hans Christian Andersen's 'Little

Mermaid'. And his cousin George's RAF joke, about what are a mermaid's vital statistics ... 38-22-1/6d. a pound!

But he wished there *were* mermaids. He had a daydream about coming into the cave and surprising one, combing her long blonde hair down to half conceal her rosy breasts, like in fairy-tale books or the photos from the Windmill Theatre. It would be nice to ... his mind always sheered away from what would be nice to do with her.

Ah, well. No mermaids now. Just war souvenirs. You couldn't have everything, and already today had been better than Christmas. Still, he'd look inside, like he always had. Might be a lump of Jerry aeroplane or something ...

There was *something*. Something long and pale, stretched out. Almost like a person lying there ...

Barmy! Things always changed into something else, when you walked right up to them boldly. But that could almost be a long leg, a long bare leg, as shapely as the girls' at the Windmill.

He shot upright so hard, he banged his head painfully on the rock roof. But when he opened his eyes after the agony, she was still there. The Mermaid. Her hair was gracefully swirled across the pebbles, the way the sea had left her. Her wide grey eyes were looking straight at him, with an air of appeal. Her face was pale, but quite untouched. She'd been wearing a dress, but there wasn't that much left of it. Just enough to pass the censors at the Windwill.

Transfixed, he slowly reached out and touched her. Her face was cold. Not human cold, like when somebody comes in from a winter's day, or has been bathing. No, she was as cold as a vase full of flowers. As cold as a thing that is not alive.

Dead. But death and the sea had been kind to her; and to him. Nothing had touched her except the thing that had killed her. If there had been blood, the sea had washed it away on her voyage ashore. She was dead, but she was entirely beautiful. She was beautiful, but entirely dead. On the beautiful pebbles of the cave, with her hair around her. No smell but the clean smell of the sea. She might have been a lovely ship's figure-head, washed ashore after a shipwreck.

He just stood and stared and stared. She must have come off some ship. What was she? Norwegian, Dutch, Danish? Sometimes their coasters carried the captain's wife and family.

He was there a long time. Somehow he knew that once he moved, nothing would ever be the same again. She would change into something else, like the piece of wood that wasn't a bird; like the minefield that wasn't really a minefield.

He would have liked to take her home.

He would like to have kept her here, and come to see her often.

But he was a realist in the end. He remembered the cods' heads on the rocks. Once he moved, they would put her in a hole in the ground. Once he moved, she would only exist on the written form. And she was so beautiful, here in her cave …

He might have stayed … how long? But he heard the roar of the waves; the roar of the returning tide. He ran out in a panic. Waves were starting to stream up the beach, and the dog was nowhere to be seen.

He began to run up the beach. There was a khaki-clad figure on the cliff, striding to and fro on sentry-duty. Brian waved and shouted, and then began to cry as he ran.

He had no idea why he was crying. All the rest of his life, he could never quite work out why he had been crying.

Notes for Going Up

Summary
This first-person narrative, told by a football fan, looks at the excitement of following a football team that has a chance of being promoted. However, it also examines the darker side of football hooliganism and shows how easy it is to be swept up in violence which is none of your making. Apart from all that, it also has a surprising twist at the end. See if you can guess it.

What do you think?
This story is told from one person's point of view in their own words and uses a lot of colloquial language. In spite of this, some very serious points about gangs and peer pressure are made. As you read the story, think about:

- the examples of slang and colloquial English included and what effect this language has on the story
- how the excitement about the possible promotion of Barfax Town is shown
- the way 'The Ointment' gang is described.

Questions
Back up your answers with quotations or references to the story.
1. Why does Tel have to go to the match with Dale?
2. Describe Tel's journey to the match.
3. What attitude does Tel have towards the gang and how does it change?
4. How does Dale react at the end of the story?
5. This story has a surprise at the end. Give reasons why you did or did not guess it.

Further activity
Write the newspaper article that reports on both the promotion of Barfax Town and Lud's death.

- Check the layout of newspaper articles and choose a headline, sub-headings and a picture.
- Collect appropriate sports vocabulary by reading football newspaper articles.
- Plan out the sequence of events and include eyewitness interviews.

Going Up

It was going to be the most exciting day of my life when Barfax Town played Lincoln City away in the last game of the season. If we won, Barfax would be promoted to the First Division for the first time since my dad was a kid. The whole town buzzed with it for a fortnight. You could feel the tension, just walking through the streets.

We had our tickets and seats on the coach. Dad and me, I mean. We never went to away matches but we were off to this one, no danger. Part-time supporters Dale always calls us, but it's not that. Dad works Saturday mornings so it's impossible for him to get away in time. He'd got special permission this time though, like a lot of other guys in Barfax.

Dale's my brother. He's a red-hot Town supporter. Goes to every match, but not with Dad and me. He's sixteen and part of the Ointment. The Ointment are the Barfax headbangers, feared by every club in the land according to him. Dad reckons they're a bunch of tossers and Dale should kick 'em into touch but he won't. Dead loyal to Lud, see? Lud Hudson, leader of the Ointment and cock of the Barfax Kop.

Was, I should say. *Was* loyal, till all that stuff went down at Lincoln. A right mess, that was. Total bummer. If you're not doing anything special I'll tell you all about it.

First thing was, Dad lost his half day off. Big job came in at work and that was that. 'Sorry, Tel,' he goes. 'Can't be helped.'

My name's Terry but everybody calls me Tel. And yes I *know* I should've said, 'Ah well, it's only a game,' but I didn't. I went ballistic instead. Well, this was Thursday, right? *Two*

71

flipping days before the match, and I'd been building up to it for a fortnight. 'S'not fair,' I screeched. 'Everyone else is off, why not me? Our Dale's going.'

And that's when I got this brilliant idea. I could go with Dale, couldn't I? I eyeballed Dad through my tears. 'Why can't *Dale* take me – he's my brother, isn't he?' You could see he wasn't keen. Dad, I mean. He sighed, pulled a face.

'Our Dale … he's not *reliable*, Tel. It's those headbangers he knocks around with. I wouldn't feel easy in my mind …'

Easy in your mind? Wow, did I let rip. What about *my* mind? What about I've been looking forward to this match for *two weeks*? Why should *I* stay home while all my mates're there, shouting for the Town? They'll show off, Monday. Laugh at me. I won't dare show my face at school.

And he gave in. Against his better judgement, he said, but I didn't care. I was over the moon.

Our Dale wasn't. He went ape-shape. *'Tel?'* he yelps when Dad mentions it. 'Drag our *Tel* along? You're joking. My mates. Lud … I'll be a laughing stock, Dad. They'll *crucify* me.'

Poor old Dad. Not only was he missing the match himself, he was getting all this grief from the two of us as well. Don't think I'll have any kids when *I* grow up. Anyway, he lays into our Dale, tells him at sixteen it's time he started taking a bit of responsibility and all that, and in the end the big plonker agrees to take me. No choice really.

So. The big day rolled round at last, and at half eleven there I was in my Town scarf and cap, trotting at my brother's heels towards the coach park. He was going fast on purpose but I wasn't bothered. I'd have stuck with him somehow if he'd been Lynford flipping *Christie*. The road was crammed with folk in scarves and caps, all heading the same way. I bet most of 'em had never been to a match before in their lives.

You should've seen the coach park. Talk about seething. There must've been at least twelve coaches, and that's not counting all the people who were going by train or car. Dale heads straight for the Ointment coach. They don't have their own, I don't mean that, but they must've planned in advance to take one over because there they were in a mob by the door, shouting and laughing, stopping other folk from getting near. I don't suppose many people fancied travelling with them anyway.

'Hey up, Dale – started a day nursery, have you?' A great husky guy in black, studded leather looks from Dale to me and back to Dale.

My brother grins, sheepishly. 'Naw, just minding our Tel for the day. You know how it is.'

'You mean … Tel here's travelling with *us*?'

'Well, yeah, just this once. My old man …'

'Sod your old man. What if …?'

'Hey, mind your language, Lud. I'll just have to … you know … stay out of it if it happens, that's all.'

'Stay *out* of it?' He scowled at my brother. Others were chuckling, nudging one another. I wished Dad was with us. 'Now you listen here, my son. You stay out today, you're *out*, geddit? Ointment don't *choose* when to rumble. Ointment's there for its mates, for the *Town*, see? Town pride, is what it's all about. You think about that all the way down, son, 'cause there ain't no *nannies* in the Ointment.'

He was great, that Lud. I mean, I *know* he was a thug, but you should've seen how he controlled those headbangers. They *worshipped* him. Nobody else could've done it.

It was terrific, that coach ride. See – to really enjoy a match there's got to be atmosphere, and those guys really knew how to build atmosphere. It was the jokes and the songs, especially the songs. What they did was, they started yelling for the kids in various parts of the bus to give them a song. You know – *back seat back seat sing us a song, back seat – sing us a song*. The kids on the back seat would sing a song, then it'd be, *front end front end sing us a song* – and so on. Just after Doncaster we ran over a dog, and like a flash they crowded up to the back window going, *dead dog dead dog sing us a song* – horrible I know, but magic too. I've never felt so fired up in my life.

We got to Lincoln just after one. The police were waiting to escort the Town fans, but Lud knew an alleyway and the Ointment slipped into it. Dale had ignored me on the coach and he ignored me now. I had to run to keep up as they negotiated the alley and headed for a pub they knew opposite the ground.

I'd never been in a pub. I didn't know kids could. I plucked at Dale's sleeve. 'I can't go in there. I don't want to.'

'Shut it, kid. You're with me, you go where I go. Come on.'

The place was packed. Smoky. They barged in, shouting and swearing, intimidating customers into making room for them. Nobody took any notice of me, it was like I wasn't there. All these bodies jostling, shoving me around. I couldn't see over them. It was taking me all my time to keep from falling. I was sweating like a pig and the smell of the place made me feel sick.

After a bit they found some seats – I think people left to get away from us – and Dale put me on a bench between two of the guys. He'd got me a Coke and some crisps. I thought, this is better. It's going to be all right now. They were talking about the match. Next season in the first division. Cheering and laughing, slurping pints. Dale had given over telling them to mind their language. I sat there and tried to be part of the Ointment.

It might have been OK if a crowd of Lincoln fans hadn't showed up. Twenty-past two and in they came in their colours, roaring. They knew we were there, and the Ointment had been expecting them. They leapt up, overturning chairs, knocking glasses and beermats on the floor, surging towards their challengers. In a second I went from being crammed in to having the whole bench to myself. I didn't know what I was supposed to do. *You're with me – you go where I go.* Was I meant to join the fight?

It *was* a fight, over there by the door. A terrible fight. Crashing and yelling and the sound of things breaking. The customers had fled out the back. There was just the fight, and a guy behind the bar on the phone, and me. I couldn't move. I sat there wishing I'd stayed home. I didn't care about the match any more, I just wanted to be somewhere familiar. Somewhere safe.

There was a noise, over the noise of fighting. Sirens. The Ointment and the Lincoln lads crammed the doorway, struggling to get out of the pub while continuing to knock hell out of one another. I looked for Dale but couldn't see him. He'd forgotten me. I was alone in a city I didn't know. A city full of enemies.

Suddenly the pub was empty. A guy charged over a sea of broken glass, aimed a kick at a youth in the doorway and the pair of them swayed snarling out of sight. I slipped off the bench and ran to the door, yelling for my brother. Two police cars stood at the kerb, blue lights flashing. The fight was a few metres away down the street. A woman somewhere screamed.

Dogs came out of a white van. Police dogs on leads, pulling their handlers towards the battle. The fighters broke and ran, all except one who stood bent over, blood pouring from between the fingers he'd clamped to his face. It wasn't Dale. I started in the direction the fight had gone because I didn't know what else to do. I had my ticket, but I couldn't remember where the coaches were picking us up after. How could I watch a soccer match, knowing I was lost a hundred miles from home?

It was then I heard my name. 'Terry? What're you doing here? Where's your dad?' I turned, weak with relief. It was Popo, Dad's mate, with Danny his son, same age as me.

I shook my head. 'Dad couldn't come. Work. I'm with Dale, but he's …' I gestured towards the dog-handlers. 'He's somewhere, fighting.'

'Oh, I see. Oh dear. Well, you'd better come with us, I think. Never know when Dale might … got a ticket, have you?'

'Yes.' I got it out, showed him. I'd never been so pleased to see anyone in my life.

He nodded, smiled. 'Come on then. We'll see Dale inside, I expect.'

We didn't though. Popo sat me and Danny on a rail so we could see over people's heads, and all through the match I kept looking round for my brother, except the last ten minutes when it got too nail-biting and I forgot. They were torture, those last ten minutes. We seemed to be heading for a goalless draw – missing out on promotion by two rotten points – when a Lincoln player fouled Billy Watson and the ref awarded Town a free kick just outside the box. Watson took it himself and it was a beauty, swerving round the end of their wall and ricocheting off the underside of the bar into the top right hand corner of the net. Half a centimetre higher and it'd have bounced out. You should've heard us roar. You probably *did* – it's only a hundred miles after all. Anyway there were ten minutes left and they chucked everything at us. I'm not kidding – even their *goalie* had a shot. Well, they'd nothing to lose and everything to gain, but it was no use. Our lads hung on and that's how we went up.

Popo drove me home. Danny and I clamped our scarves in the windows so they flapped in the slipstream all the way up the A1.

That's the good news. The bad news is that Dale didn't make it home that night, and poor Lud didn't make it at all. Somebody stabbed him and he died in hospital without ever knowing the result of the match. None of the Ointment saw the game. By the time Watson swerved us into Division One they were all down the police station being charged. It was Sunday lunchtime when our Dale turned up. He'd come by train, and he was breathing funny owing to bruised ribs. Dad had intended giving him hell for leaving me, but he looked so rough he let him stagger off to bed.

Monday teatime we're all in the front room watching telly. Town on an open top bus getting a civic reception, but when the chairman comes on our Dale gets up and leaves the room because he knows what he's going to say. Naturally he starts by regretting Lud's tragic death, but then he says, 'Those youths who brawled on the streets of Lincoln last Saturday are not our supporters. They have no share in our triumph and are not welcome on our terraces. We are a First Division club with First Division fans. There is no place in our ranks for scum.'

A bit later on I go up to the toilet and pass Dale on the landing and he's been crying. 'Have I heck,' he says when I mention it, but he has. He's had the telly on in his room and heard the whole thing. Just can't admit it to his little sister, that's all.

Anyway, all this was last season. *This* season he's a different guy. He goes to every match same as before, only he doesn't stand with the Ointment. He doesn't stand with me and Dad either, but that's all right. He's *grown*, see? Just like Barfax Town.

Notes for Charlotte's Wanderers

Summary
The happiness the narrator feels at going out with his first girlfriend rapidly disappears when he discovers that she can't come out because she has to ... play football! This story explores the highs and lows of relationships as well as showing what the narrator learns about himself.

What do you think?
The boy in this story helps Charlotte to improve her footballing skills and the main thrust of the story is Charlotte's determination to improve. As you read the story, think about the following:

- What is Charlotte's excuse for not turning up to a date later on in the story?
- How does Charlotte show how keen she is to improve her skill in football?
- What does she say most people think of female football teams?
- What does her boyfriend think of female footballers at the end of the story?

Questions
Back up your answers with quotations or references to the story.

1. Which video do they watch on their first date?
2. How does the boy help Charlotte to head the ball?
3. How does he embarrass her at the next match?
4. What mistakes does he make in the last match and what does he learn from it?
5. What do you think is the author's point of view about female football teams and players?

Further activity
Role-play a scene where the boy in the story (you'll have to give him a name!) is talking about Charlotte's football team to a group of friends who don't think girls should play football.

- Think of which arguments for and against women's football you are going to use.
- Check how you should set out the script.
- Try to use some words and phrases which the boy uses in the story.

Charlotte's Wanderers

We met at PriceRite supermarket. I'd been working there some time stacking shelves on Thursday evenings after school. She was a new girl and I was given the job of showing her what to do on her first day. She wore the supermarket's green overalls, a plastic badge saying *Charlotte*, and a big smile which made her lips go all crinkly round the edges.

I'd never had a girlfriend before but I knew Charlotte was my number one choice. By week four of her shelf-stacking shifts I was ready.

'Do you … er fancy … watching a video?' I said, trying to make my voice sound real calm.

'What video?'

'Er … *Vaults of Terror 2*?'

'Seen it.'

'*Braindead 3*.'

'I heard it was boring.'

'Oh,' I said, still trying to keep cool.

There was a pause. I looked up at her round the side of a stack of boxes of special-offer chocolate biscuits. She gave me a crinkly smile.

'Laurel and Hardy?' she said.

'Yeah!'

'Really?'

'Why not?'

It was agreed we would meet at her house on Saturday for a session of video viewing. I did wheelies up and down the pavements all the way home that Thursday evening, not minding a bit that I really hated Laurel and Hardy. The countdown to my first serious date had already begun and there were only 2,580 minutes to go until Saturday at three o'clock.

We had a whole month of video watching. Four glorious weeks of zombie terror and Laurel and Hardy. In the fifth week I went up to her house as usual. Her dad opened the door and said she was out.

'Didn't you know?' he said. 'She's gone to football.'

'Gone to football?' I repeated.

'Yes.'

I opened and closed my mouth in silence like a demented zombie from the video we wouldn't be watching. Her dad started to close the door and I knew I had to find something else to say to him to try and make sense of what was happening.

'I didn't know she liked watching football,' I said. Her dad gave me a hard look.

'You've got it wrong,' he said. 'She isn't *watching* football, she's playing it. Down on Park Grove.'

With that he was gone and the door was closed. I walked down their drive and sat on my bike. Charlotte was *playing football*. Why hadn't she told me about it?

I looked back towards their house, hoping that Charlotte would suddenly open the door and come running out saying it was only a joke. Only she didn't. The house looked still and empty.

I peered down at my handlebars. They were pointing in the direction of Park Grove. It would be a long cycle, ten miles at least, and most of it uphill. But if I started now I could be there before the game was finished. Maybe see a fair bit of the second half if I pedalled hard.

Then I was off. Down Packer Lane, onto the cinder track, over the railway bridge and out onto the main road and making good time. Round the big round-about and into ... I stopped. Pulled my brakes on hard. Of course. I was so stupid. Really thick. Charlotte wasn't playing football down Park Grove. No way. Not her. It was the push-off. An excuse. She'd had enough of me. Fed up with Saturday video watching and she hadn't the guts to tell me herself. She'd got her dad to do the dirty work for her. I turned the bike round and slowly, very slowly, made my way back home.

I dreaded Thursday. I thought of not going to work. Perhaps I could phone in saying I'd got the flu. But I needed the money – with Christmas coming along there were loads of presents to buy. Still, there was one big present I didn't have to worry about any longer.

I saw her straight away, coming out of the stockroom. She came towards me.

'We need to talk,' she said and tugged the sleeve of my overall, starting to pull me back towards the stockroom. Only Mrs Hillett came along and saw us and pointed towards 'Confectionery and Household'. When Mrs Hillett points her skinny finger you move – if you want to keep your job that is.

It was finishing time before we had a chance to meet. Charlotte waited for me in the car park.

'Sorry about Saturday,' she said.

'I thought we were finished,' I said.

'Of course not ... I just didn't have a chance to tell you. It all happened so fast. The team were short of a player and I couldn't let them down. I tried to phone.'

A rusty old van with its front bumper tied on with rope pulled into the car park and started to honk its horn.

'That's Marie ... I've got to go. It's training tonight.'

'But ...'

Charlotte waved in the direction of the van.

'I'd better go,' she said. Then she kissed me and ran off. Just before she got to the van she turned and shouted.

'Come on Saturday. To the match. It's at Park Grove ... three o'clock kick-off.'

I could taste her kiss for days. It lured me on like a magnet to Park Grove. I decided I didn't want to appear too keen, too desperate to see her, so I got there at half-time.

The teams were in huddles at opposite ends of the pitch sucking bits of orange. One huddle was in a blue strip, the other in yellow and black. I searched both huddles for the head of ginger hair and crinkly smile that belonged to Charlotte. She was in the middle of the blue shirts, only she wasn't smiling but listening very hard to a thin woman who was giving them all some grief. I could see this must be Marie from the rusty van. They were obviously losing.

Then a whistle went, Marie collected in the bits of leftover oranges and the two teams changed ends ready to begin the second half.

The next forty-five minutes were a disaster. Marie ran up and down the touchline just like my dad used to when I played in the junior school football team, only Marie ran faster and shouted louder. In fact much louder. It all came out in a garbled gabble like a neverending stream:

'Kik it tout. Kik it tout. Tout tout tout. CrossitEllen. CrossitEllen. StopitJo. Passitpassit. Upup. Up pup pup. ChaseitLin. Chaseit. Kikittoutkikittouttouttouttout.'

She didn't stop for forty-five minutes. It made my head hurt listening to her.

All her shouting and running were a waste of time. They lost three-nil. The more she shouted the worse they played. The backs were forward when they should have been back, and the forwards were back when they should have been forward. The goalie let in the softest goal by looking at Marie when she should have been looking at the ball. In the last ten minutes of the match they truly lived up to their names of 'The Women's Wanderers' by wandering about all over the pitch without any sense of purpose or direction.

As the final whistle blew and all the players started to leave the pitch I wondered if it was best for me to slip away quietly on my bike and head for home. But my feet were rooted to the ground and I couldn't move. Charlotte looked at me for the first time that afternoon and shook her head. I reckoned she was ready to burst into tears. Then Marie gathered them all up in another huddle and I knew it was time to climb onto my saddle and head off home.

I was woken early the next morning. Somebody was knocking on our back door. The somebody was Charlotte, still dressed in her football gear. I went down to let her in.

'Marie says we should have extra practice. I thought you'd help me.'

'But it's half past eight on a Sunday morning!'

'So?'

We went down to a bit of waste ground by the scrapyard and began to kick a ball about.

'We've got to work ... at the ... midfield linkage,' said Charlotte between kicks. 'Not getting caught ... in the ... offside trap ... that's what Marie tells us ... in her team talk.'

I trapped the ball hard with my foot.

'Talk is OK,' I said. 'But ...'

'But what?'

I spun round with the ball at my feet. Charlotte started to kick at my ankles, trying to hit the ball away.

'Talk is OK,' I repeated, 'but it's skill that counts.' She lashed out with her foot, barged me with her shoulder and as I fell to the ground she grabbed the ball with her hands.

'Like that skill?' she shouted and began to hit me with the ball. 'You think we're crap, don't you? Mr Clever Boots ... Think just because we're a women's team we can't play decent football.'

She was hitting me harder and harder with the ball.

'You men ... think you know it all ... We'll show you ...'

I took the ball from her and said quietly, 'I was just trying to say ...'

'Well, don't.'

She grabbed the ball again and ran off to kick it angrily against the wire fence of the scrapyard. I picked myself up from the ground and watched her, pleased I wasn't the wire fence. I'd had enough dents and bashes for one Sunday morning.

When her anger had started to die down a bit I went over.

'What about heading?'

She just carried on kicking and ignored me.

'How's your heading?' I said.

'It's fine … It's just you who's doing my head in … all you men …' she said and kicked the ball viciously at me.

Her heading was poor. In fact she couldn't head the ball at all, but I didn't make any comment about it. Every time I threw the ball in the air she ran to head it and then pulled away at the last minute and missed it by a mile. Then I remembered an old tactic my dad used to try.

'Jump' I said.

'What?'

'Jump in the air as high as you can.'

'But we're supposed to be trying heading.'

'Yeah … and it's all part of it … to build confidence. Jump on the spot as high as you can. Come on – go for it.'

For the next ten minutes we jumped about like two crazed kangaroos till we could jump no more. Then I took hold of the ball and held it up to her forehead.

'Knock it out of my hands.'

'What?'

'Just do it.'

After three goes I held the ball further from her forehead and we repeated the exercise. Each time she hit the ball hard and true with her forehead. Then I began to throw the ball very gently in the air and again she hit it true. I threw it higher.

'Head through the ball … through it.' And so she did.

'Now we'll put the two together … I'm going to throw it really high … You leap in the air and head it … Right?'

'Right.'

I threw, she leapt, the ball missed her head and hit her smack on her nose. She fell to the ground and blood trickled out of her nose, down her face and onto her shirt. I ran over in a panic towards her. Down on the floor her face was screwed up in pain.

'Charlotte … are you all right?' I cried.

She looked up at me and her face broke into a smile. She got up and began to wipe away the blood from her face and shirt. I wanted us to take a break and go back home for a bit of easy TV cartoon watching but she was having none of it.

'No,' she said. 'I'm going to get this sorted.'

And sorted it was. I threw the ball high, she hit it in the middle of her forehead and the ball sailed up in the air over the wire fence and into the scrapyard.

'One-nil,' she shouted. 'One-bloomin'-nil.' And she jumped higher in the air than any kangaroo or Man U player ever has. I looked at her in a gobsmacked sort of way.

'Now we're ready,' she said. 'Ready for our next match.'

The next match was different. For a start there was no Marie hurtling down the touchline shouting abuse at twenty zillion decibels. Apparently she'd had to go away on business up north. I reckoned she'd given up on The Women's Wanderers and gone to give some other poor team the benefit of her 90-minute verbal abuse and touchline torment.

There was a thick fog as the teams kicked off, and total

silence. I strained my eyes and ears to be sure there really were twenty-two players out there and that they hadn't cleared off to the changing rooms to leave me standing alone like a lonely lemon. The occasional sound of the ref's whistle and lurching ghostly grey half-figures appearing and then disappearing in and out of the fog were the sum total of my impressions of the first half.

At half-time the two teams didn't dare stand too far apart in their orange-sucking huddles in case they never found each other again. There was talk of abandoning the game. It seemed as if all our Sunday-morning, blood-bursting, head-throbbing efforts down by the scrapyard were in vain. The ref had her head in the rule book trying to work out what to do in the event of a fog-logged game, when the fog started to thin under the heat of a feeble December sun. Strands of the fog swirled about and began to drift off in the direction of both goals, leaving the middle of the pitch in clear air. The match was saved and the second half began.

Most of the early play was in the Wanderers' half with a gaggle of players all scrabbling about near the goalmouth. At least I *think* it was a gaggle playing football and not doing a spot of disco dancing – the fog was still pretty thick around that part of the pitch. Then there was a shout, a whistle, a cheer and the Wanderers were one-nil down.

Straight from the kick-off the play switched to the opposition's goalmouth with a repeat of the disco dancing impressions. I ran down the touchline to get a closer look and was just near enough to see the ball skid off an opposition boot for a Wanderers' corner. I ran round behind the goal as the corner kick was fired high into the air close to goal. A little gaggle of blue and red shirts jumped high in the air, their heads strained towards the spinning ball. Defenders and attackers clawed for dominance, each eager to make first contact with the ball.

There was no fog now, only one ginger head millimetres higher then the rest. One straining attacker so close to the ball. Her head pulled back, poised to strike, and ... missed. Yes, missed the ball completely.

The gaggle slumped downwards. All heads failed to make contact with their target. Bodies sagged groundwards. Yet the ball fell too and brushed the shoulder of a downwards attacker. Almost in slow motion it spun towards the black mesh of the goal net. A lunging hand of the goalkeeper moved towards the ball. But the ball seemed to have a will and life of its own and flipped over the despairing outstretched gloved fingers to land firmly in the back of the net.

I was so proud of her. I was really really proud of Charlotte the footballer who had scored the goal to save the match in its dying seconds. Her strike was the one dazzle of sunlight which had cut through the foggy gloom of a December day. She told me to cut the crap.

'Stop going on about it, will you.'

'But it was your first goal for the club ... and what a goal.'

'Yeah ... I missed the header.'

'They all count.'

'A fluke.'

'Never ... Sunday practice by the scrapyard pays dividend in the Saturday thriller.'

'Just shut up, will you.'

I couldn't. I wouldn't. For the whole week I had my head in the stars. We watched a video of the 1966 World Cup Final on Saturday night with the sound turned down so we could add our own commentary. Sunday was scrapyard practice, concentrating on free kick tactics. Monday was football magazine reading with insights into international stardom. And Tuesday ... Well, Tuesday we had a row. Charlotte said she'd had enough of blooming football and if I as much as mentioned the word we were finished. So Tuesday and Wednesday I did a bit of private artistic preparation for the Saturday match in the way of banner painting.

The result of my efforts was a big sign with blue and black writing on a sheet smuggled out of the black bedroom saying

KICK IT UP
HEAD IT IN
CHARLOTTE

On Thursday I dribbled a can of baked beans round the legs of six customers, three shopping trolleys, down the frozen foods and dairy produce aisle, only to be given a yellow card and the warning of a full season suspension by Mrs Hillett. Some refs just want to spoil the game by their interfering stoppages. They should be encouraging young talent and a free-flowing end-to-end match. What the spectators want to see is the can being kicked right through the storeroom doorway to the cheers of the customers. But what do we get instead? Penalty after penalty and the wagging bony finger.

On Friday Charlotte found the banner and ripped it up, saying I'd 'really lost it' and if I ever brought anything along like that she'd walk off the pitch and never speak to me again. But I didn't mind. I was in good spirits and maybe the banner would have been difficult to fix to my bike for the ride to Park Grove.

On Saturday there was only one thing that mattered. One 90-minute, action-packed, ball-rolling, crowd-cheering, goal-scoring, titanic battle of skill, endeavour and daring. Yes! The Wanderers were once again gracing the turf of Park Grove.

Charlotte said it was only a friendly after several weeks of league matches, but I said, 'Friendly it may be, but it's still the chance to keep on the goal-scoring road. The pathway to success is only open to those with twinkling feet, hearts of oak and heads of steel.'

Charlotte said it should be a relaxed match and a bit of fun.

Marie was once again conspicuous by her absence. She'd sent the team a postcard with a picture of Old Trafford on it and a brief message saying: *Am talent spotting in the north. Back soon. Marie.*

The postmark was a bit smudged but it looked like Basingstoke which was only eight miles away. You certainly wouldn't find much talent in Basingstoke and it was south of us, not north.

I decided I'd do a mini-Marie. Not a 90-minute mobile verbal but a bit of encouragement on the touchline. The Wanderers needed support and the match crowd was small. In fact, it was microscopic. There were two sets of parents sitting in cars, a scruffy-looking dog with one ear, and me. Things certainly needed livening up.

I needn't have worried. For this was going to be one of the liveliest Saturday afternoons at Park Grove for some time.

It all began when the opposition, the Giants, ran out of the changing rooms and onto the pitch. You could see why the team got their name. Two of them were the biggest and tallest girls I have ever seen. One must have been nearly as tall as Blackpool Tower and the other, her twin, was even taller. She looked as tall as the Eiffel Tower. I felt dizzy just looking up at them both. The ground shook as they ran onto the pitch. The dog with one ear cocked his head on one side, barked and ran off.

The team gathered round in a kind of rugby scrum with Eiffel and Blackpool in the middle like tent poles. I thought this was going to be exciting and that perhaps they'd got it all wrong and were going to play rugby. I'd never seen a match with one team playing football versus another team playing rugby before.

The Giants started to stamp their feet and shout a war cry like I once heard the New Zealand Rugby team do on TV. It was a disappointment when a few seconds later they started to kick the ball about and not pick it up and run with it.

The first incident happened after five minutes of play. The Wanderers had the ball when Eiffel stood on the foot of one of our players. It must have been like a three-ton truck running over you and the result was one limping player heading for the changing room. We were now reduced to ten and had no substitute to bring on.

Fifteen minutes later one of our star forwards, Sharon, was making a solo run towards the goal. She'd already beaten a couple of players and only Blackpool and the goalie stood between her and the goal. She made to go right, feinted and checked and clipped the ball past Blackpool on the left. All she had to do was to sprint left round Blackpool, regain control of the ball and crack it hard past the goalie. A doddle to go one-nil up.

Blackpool saw the plan just in time and lurched left. She made no attempt to play the ball and just obstructed Sharon's way. The two collided with Sharon sprinting fast. There was a nasty crunching noise and Sharon clattered to the deck, clutching her leg in agony.

Her mum came dashing out of her car, shouted abuse at Blackpool and carried Sharon off the pitch. Two minutes later her car sped out of the car park in a shower of dust and fury. It should have been the red card for Blackpool but the ref just bit her bottom lip and restarted the game. In the remainder of the half it was backing-off time. All of our players tried to keep a five-mile exclusion zone between them and the terrible tower twins.

At half-time they'd scored two goals and things looked grim. Our goalie had a sudden attack of nervousitis – I think it was called twin tower fever – and she left the pitch for the safety of the changing rooms. We now had eight players left and twin tower fever could strike again at any moment. In fact an epidemic was expected in the next three seconds.

I decided it was time for direct action and ran onto the pitch. I could be the sub, the hero to save the hour. I'd got my trainers and tracksuit on so there would be no stopping me.

Charlotte and I would team up to make searching raids into the Giants' goalmouth. We'd be fearless. The tower twins held no terror for our twinkling toes. We'd be too fast and clever for such lumbering mountains.

Charlotte wasn't keen on the idea. She pushed me back in the direction of the touchline, shouting, 'No way. This is an all girls team and men are not allowed.'

Some of the players started to giggle. Charlotte still had hold of me and was pushing me further and further back towards the touchline.

Half as a joke one player said, 'Oh, let him play.'

There were more giggles.

'It's only a friendly,' said another. Groans and a few giggles.

'Go on, Chaz, it'll be a laugh,' said a third and turned to the ref, adding, 'What about a lad playing for us?'

The ref bit her lip and shrugged her shoulders. The question was asked again to the Giants.

'Who?'

'Him!'

'Him?'

'Yeah.'

More laughs from both lots of players. It was like picking teams on the beach, and I was the leftover nobody wanted. But I'd show them. They'd see.

Blackpool Tower stepped forward and looked me over like I was a second-hand pair of socks at a jumble sale.

'Only if *it* plays in goal,' she said with a growl.

There was a cheer from the Wanderers. I began to grin. Charlotte glared at me but I knew my chance had come.

The second half started straight away. We had quite a strong wind in our favour. I knew I had to take a big kick and smack the ball down into their goalmouth. If I could do this and try not to land it within a hundred miles of either tower we could be in with a chance. The trouble was that to start with nobody wanted to kick it back to me and there was a lot of fiddling-about sort of play in the middle of the pitch. Then one of the giants hoofed it upfield towards my goal. I came running out of my area and whacked it straight back downfield. But the wind was unpredictable and a sudden gust carried it high in the air and then far off to the left. It finally landed in a row of allotments.

By the time I'd gone to collect it and play had restarted we only had twenty minutes left before the final whistle. Still the play fiddled about in midfield with the remainders of the Wanderers running about in the opposite direction to the ball, trying to avoid the towers.

At last I received a long back pass. I waited for the ball to come to me and gathered it up close to my chest. I looked round the field and noted the positions of both towers. Charlotte was well downfield. I threw the ball up in the air, drew back my foot and hit it hard and true. Up it went like a rocket and then fell close to the goalmouth. Charlotte was there like an arrow. The ball bounced for a second time and then, with a crack of her head, she hit it fiercely into the back of the net.

Yes! Yes! Yes! No shoulder glance this time but a crisp sharp header right on target. I was ecstatic and ran about in the goal like a kid who's just got his first Christmas present.

We still had enough time. Enough minutes left to win the match. With the wind still blowing hard a repeat kick was all that was needed to draw level. After that a final onslaught would surely bring us victory. What a triumph it would be to snatch a win out of the jaws of failure.

I waited for the back pass or a hoof upfield but none came. Time was running out and our chances were diminishing by the minute.

'Kick it back ... kick it back!' I screamed, but the wind drowned my cries. This was too much to bear. I knew what I had to do. It would be a risk but at this stage of the game there was no other choice.

I ran out of goal and down to the scrambling cluster of players in midfield. I tackled the first player and gained possession of the ball. I rounded a second and the goal was in sight. The towers advanced but I wasn't scared of them. My twinkling toes would be too fast for them. I feinted and dribbled, but on they came like a moving wall. All it needed was a little chip with the ball over them both and I'd be through.

I'm not sure exactly what happened next but somehow it all went wrong. I was sandwiched between the two. Squashed by Blackpool and Eiffel I fell to the ground like a burst paper bag. Blackpool had the ball at her feet. She steadied herself and drew back her foot. With enormous power she kicked the ball high over my head and into our goal – where I should have been.

I learned two things that afternoon at Park Grove – things I should have known all the time if I'd stopped to think about it.

The first was that it's no good being a selfish player, setting out to win the match single-handed. Football is a team game and if you forget that you could end up doing a nosedive on the turf like I did.

The second thing was to do with Charlotte – she was developing into a really good player. Soon she'll be playing in better teams than the Wanderers. Maybe she'll get a place in an England women's team. And what after that? The Premier Division? Once I would have thought that a ridiculous idea, but now I'm not so sure.

Notes for The Mouth-organ Boys

Summary
This short story is set in the Caribbean. All Delroy's friends have a mouth-organ and have formed a gang. They certainly don't want anyone around who hasn't got one and Delroy feels left out in the cold. At the end of the story he miraculously has a mouth-organ, but suspicions are aroused: has Delroy stolen it?

What do you think?
Delroy's longing for a mouth-organ is shown throughout the story. The author, James Berry, also shows the way this affects his relationship with his mother and his friends. As you read the story, think about the following:

- how Delroy tries to get a mouth-organ at the beginning
- the way Delroy is treated by his friends at school
- how Delroy tries to get into the 'Mouth-organ boys' gang.

Questions
Choose words and phrases from the story to back up your answers.
1. How can you tell this story is set in the Caribbean?
   a) Look for details in the story.
   b) Make a note of how people speak and compare what the characters say to the way you would say the same thing.
2. Why did the mouth-organ boys think Delroy had stolen the mouth-organ? Did you think he had?
3. Do you think having a mouth-organ would solve Delroy's problems with 'The Mouth-organ boys'? Give reasons for your answer.

Further activity
Part of this story is missing, so that the reader doesn't know until the end of the story how Delroy got the mouth-organ. Write the missing part of the story explaining how Delroy got his mouth-organ. In the story Delroy says that his mother gave him the mouth-organ, but try to brainstorm a list of other ways Delroy could have got the mouth-organ and choose the best one. You could use a spider diagram for this.

- Try to copy the style James Berry uses in his writing.
- Pick out descriptions, words and phrases in the story to give you a store of vocabulary to use.

The Mouth-organ Boys

I wanted a mouth-organ, I wanted it more than anything else in the whole world. I told my mother. She kept ignoring me but I still wanted a mouth-organ badly.

I was only a boy. I didn't have a proper job. Going to school was like a job, but nobody paid me to go to school. Again I had to say to my mother. 'Mum, will you please buy a mouth-organ for me?'

It was the first time now, that my mother stood and answered me properly. Yet listen to what my mother said. 'What d'you want a mouth-organ for?'

'All the other boys have a mouth-organ, mam,' I told her.

'Why is that so important? You don't have to have something just because others have it.'

'They won't have me with them without a mouth-organ, mam,' I said.

'They'll soon change their minds, Delroy.'

'They won't, mam. They really won't. You don't know Wildo Harris. He never changes his mind. And he never lets any other boy change his mind either.'

'Delroy, I haven't got the time to argue with you. There's no money to buy a mouth-organ. I bought you new shoes and clothes for Independence Celebrations. Remember?'

'Yes, mam.'

'Well, money doesn't come on trees.'

'No, mam.' I had to agree.

'It's school-day. The sun won't stand still for you. Go and

feed the fowls. Afterwards milk the goat. Then get yourself ready for school.'

She sent me off. I had to go and do my morning jobs.

Oh my mother never listened! She never understood anything. She always had reasons why she couldn't buy me something and it was no good wanting to talk to my dad. He always cleared off to work early.

All my friends had a mouth-organ, Wildo, Jim, Desmond, Len – everybody had one, except me. I couldn't go round with them now. They wouldn't let anybody go round with them without a mouth-organ. They were now 'The Mouth-organ Boys.' And we used to be all friends. I used to be their friend. We all used to play games together, and have fun together. Now they pushed me away.

'Delroy! Delroy!' my mother called.

I answered loudly. 'Yes, mam!'

'Why are you taking so long feeding the fowls?'

'Coming, mam.'

'Hurry up, Delroy.'

Delroy. Delroy. Always calling Delroy!

I milked the goat. I had breakfast. I quickly brushed my teeth. I washed my face and hands and legs. No time left and my mother said nothing about getting my mouth-organ. But my mother had time to grab my head and comb and brush my hair. She had time to wipe away toothpaste from my lip with her hand. I had to pull myself away and say, 'Good day, Mum.'

'Have a good day, Delroy,' she said, staring at me.

I ran all the way to school. I ran wondering if the Mouth-organ Boys would let me sit with them today. Yesterday they didn't sit next to me in class.

I was glad the boys came back. We all sat together as usual. But they teased me about not having a mouth-organ.

Our teacher, Mr Goodall, started writing on the blackboard. Everybody was whispering. And it got to everybody talking quite loudly. Mr Goodall could be really cross. Mr Goodall had big muscles. He had a moustache too. I would like to be like Mr Goodall when I grew up. But he could be really cross. Suddenly Mr Goodall turned round and all the talking stopped, except for the voice of Wildo Harris. Mr Goodall held the chalk in his hand and stared at Wildo Harris. He looked at Teacher and dried up. The whole class giggled.

Mr Goodall picked out Wildo Harris for a question. He stayed sitting and answered.

'Will you please stand up when you answer a question?' Mr Goodall said.

Wildo stood up and answered again. Mr Goodall ignored him and asked another question. Nobody answered. Mr Goodall pointed at me and called my name. I didn't know why he picked on me. I didn't know I knew the answer. I wanted to stand up slowly, to kill time. But I was there, standing. I gave an answer.

'That is correct,' Mr Goodall said.

I sat down. My forehead felt hot and sweaty, but I felt good. Then in schoolyard at recess time, Wildo joked about it. Listen to what he had to say: 'Delroy Brown isn't only a big head. Delroy Brown can answer questions with big mouth.'

'Yeh!' the gang roared, to tease me.

Then Wildo had to say, 'If only he could get a *mouth*-organ.' All the boys laughed and walked away.

I went home to lunch and as usual I came back quickly. Wildo and Jim and Desmond and Len were together, at the bench, under the palm tree. I went up to them. They were swapping mouth-organs, trying out each one. Everybody made sounds on each mouth-organ, and said something. I begged Len, I begged Desmond, I begged Jim, to let me try out their mouth-organs. I only wanted a blow. They just carried on making silly sounds on each other's mouth-organs. I begged Wildo to lend me his. He didn't even look at me.

I faced Wildo. I said, 'Look. I can do something different as a Mouth-organ Boy. Will you let me do something different?'

Boy, everybody was interested. Everybody looked at me.

'What different?' Wildo asked.

'I can play the comb,' I said.

'Oh, yeh,' Wildo said slowly.

'Want to hear it?' I asked. 'My dad taught me how to play it.'

'Yeh,' Wildo said. 'Let's hear it.' And not one boy smiled or anything. They just waited.

I took out my comb. I put my piece of tissue paper over it. I began to blow a tune on my comb and had to stop. The boys were laughing too much. They laughed so much they staggered about. Other children came up and laughed too. It was all silly, laughing at me.

I became angry. Anybody would get mad. I told them they could keep their silly Mouth-organ Boys business. I told them it only happened because Desmond's granny gave him a mouth-organ for his birthday. And it only caught on because Wildo went and got a mouth-organ too. I didn't sit with the boys in class that afternoon. I didn't care what the boys did.

I went home. I looked after my goats. Then I ate. I told my mum I was going for a walk. I went into the centre of town where I had a great surprise.

The boys were playing mouth-organs and dancing. They played and danced in the town square. Lots of kids followed the boys and danced around them.

It was great. All four boys had the name 'The Mouth-organ Boys' across their chests. It seemed they did the name themselves. They cut out big coloured letters for the words from newspapers and magazines. They gummed the letters down on a strip of brown paper, then they made a hole at each end of the paper. Next a string was pushed through the holes, so they could tie the names round them. The boys looked great. What a super name: 'The Mouth-organ Boys'! How could they do it without me!

'Hey, boys!' I shouted, and waved. 'Hey, boys!' They saw me. They jumped up more with a bigger act, but ignored me. I couldn't believe Wildo, Jim, Desmond and Len enjoyed themselves so much and didn't care about me.

I was sad, but I didn't follow them. I hung about the garden railings, watching. Suddenly I didn't want to watch any more. I went home slowly. It made me sick how I didn't have a mouth-organ. I didn't want to eat. I didn't want the lemonade and bun my mum gave me. I went to bed.

Mum thought I wasn't well. She came to see me. I didn't want any fussing about. I shut my eyes quickly. She didn't want to disturb me. She left me alone. I opened my eyes again.

If I could drive a truck I could buy loads of mouth-organs. If I was a fisherman I could buy a hundred mouth-organs. If I was an aeroplane pilot I could buy truck-loads of mouth-organs. I was thinking all those things and didn't know when I fell asleep.

Next day at school The Mouth-organ Boys sat with me. I didn't know why but we just sat together and joked a little bit. I felt good running home to lunch in the usual bright sunlight.

I ran back to school. The Mouth-organ Boys were under the palm tree, on the bench. I was really happy. They were really unhappy and cross and this was very strange.

Wildo grabbed me and held me tight. 'You thief!' he said.

The other boys came around me. 'Let's search him,' they said.

'No, no!' I said. 'No.'

'I've lost my mouth-organ and you have stolen it,' Wildo said.

'No,' I said. 'No.'

'What's bulging in your pocket, then?'

'It's mine,' I told them. 'It's mine.'

The boys held me. They took the mouth-organ from my pocket.

'It's mine,' I said. But I saw myself up to Headmaster. I saw myself getting caned. I saw myself disgraced.

Wildo held up the mouth-organ. 'Isn't this red mouth-organ mine?'

'Of course it is,' the boys said.

'It's mine,' I said. 'I got it at lunchtime.'

'Just at the right time, eh?,' Desmond said.

'Say you borrowed it,' Jim said.

'Say you were going to give it back,' Len said.

Oh, I had to get a mouth-organ just when Wildo lost his! 'My mother gave it to me at lunchtime,' I said.

'Well, come and tell Teacher,' Wildo said.

Bell rang. We hurried to our class. My head was aching. My hands were sweating. My mother would have to come to school, and I hated that.

Wildo told our teacher I stole his mouth-organ. It was no good telling Teacher it was mine, but I did. Wildo said his mouth-organ was exactly like that. And I didn't have a mouth-organ.

Mr Goodall went to his desk. And Mr Goodall brought back Wildo's grubby red mouth-organ. He said it was found on the floor.

How could Wildo compare his dirty red mouth-organ with my new, my beautiful, my shining clean mouth-organ? Mr Goodall made Wildo Harris say he was sorry.

Oh it was good. It was good to become one of 'The Mouth-organ Boys'.

Notes for Fathers' Day

Summary
This story is set in modern-day America and the theme is the relationship a father has with his son. Invited to his son's school to attend a special lesson, the father is very reluctant to go, but when he gets there he goes through a series of different emotions. He hears several boys read out essays about their fathers and learns a valuable lesson from his own son.

What do you think?
This story is set in an American school but the boys' descriptions of their fathers could seem very familiar. The feelings of the father, George Adams, are described in great detail and lead you to consider family relationships. As you read, think about the following:
- How does the father behave? What do you think of him?
- How are Satterlee's mother and sisters described?
- Is the school very different to yours? In what ways?

Questions
Choose words and phrases from the story to back up your answers.
1. Make a list of details which show this story is set in America.
2. What impression do you get of the father, George Adams, at the beginning of the story? Why?
3. How is the school described?
4. What is George's reaction when he realises what the boys have been writing about?
5. Explain why George is surprised by what his son writes.
6. What is the author saying about relationships between fathers and sons? This story was written some time ago. Do you think things have changed since it was written?

Further activity
Imagine George goes back home and tells his wife about his experience at school in Bobby's class. Pick out the important details from the story:
- how George feels about going to the school
- his changing emotions once he is in the classroom
- how he reacts to his son's writing.

Fathers' Day

George Adams finished his coffee, mashed out his cigarette in the saucer, and stood up. 'I'm off,' he said to his wife as he went to the coat closet. 'See you around six.'

'Don't forget Bobby's school,' she said.

Adams stopped, and looked at her. 'What about it?' he asked.

'They're having Fathers' Day,' she said. 'Remember?'

'Oh, my God,' Adams said. He paused, then said hurriedly, 'I can't make it. It's out of the question.'

'You've got to,' she said. 'You missed it last year, and he was terribly hurt. Just go for a few minutes, but you've *got* to do it. I promised him I'd remind you.'

Adams drew a deep breath and said nothing.

'Bobby said you could just come for English class,' Eleanor went on. 'Between twelve twenty and one. Please don't let him down again.'

'Well, I'll try,' Adams said. 'I'll make it if I can.'

'It won't hurt you to do it. All the other fathers do.'

'I'm sure they do,' Adams said. He put on his hat and went out and rang for the elevator.

Eleanor came to the front door. 'No excuses, now!' she said.

'I said I'd do it if I could,' Adams replied. 'That's all I can promise you.'

Adams arrived at the school about twelve thirty, and an attendant at the door reached out to take his hat. 'No, thanks,' Adams said, clutching it firmly. 'I'm just going to be a few minutes.' He looked around and saw the cloakroom, piled high with hats and topcoats, and beyond that the auditorium, in which a number of men and boys were already having lunch. 'Maybe I'm too late,' he thought hopefully. 'Maybe the classes are already over.' To the attendant, he said, 'Do you know where I'd find the sixth grade now? They're having English, I think.'

'The office'll tell you,' the attendant said. 'Second floor.'

Adams ascended a steel-and-concrete stairway to the second floor and, through the closed doors around him, heard the high, expressionless voices of reciting boys and the lower, softly precise voices of the teachers, and as he passed the open door of an empty room, he caught the smell of old wood and chalk dust and library paste. He found the office, and a middle-aged woman there directed him to a room on the floor above, and he went up and stood outside the door for a moment, listening. He could hear a teacher's voice, and the teacher was talking about the direct object and the main verb and the predicate adjective.

After hesitating a few seconds, Adams turned the knob and quietly opened the door. The first face he saw was that of his son, in the front row, and Bobby winked at him. Then Adams looked at the thin, dark-haired teacher, who seemed a surprisingly young man. He obviously had noticed Bobby's wink, and he smiled and said, 'Mr Adams.' Adams tiptoed to the back of the room and joined about six other fathers, who were sitting in various attitudes of discomfort on a row of folding chairs. He recognised none of them, but they looked at him in a friendly way and he smiled at them,

110

acknowledging the bond of uneasiness that held them momentarily together.

The teacher was diagramming a sentence on the blackboard, breaking it down into its component parts by means of straight and oblique lines, and Adams, looking at the diagram, realised that, if called upon, he would be hard put to it to separate the subject from the predicate, and he prayed that the teacher wouldn't suffer a fit of whimsy and call on the fathers. As it turned out, the students were well able to handle the problem, and Adams was gratified to hear his son give correct answers to two questions that were put to him. 'I'll be damned,' Adams thought. 'I never got the impression he knew all that.'

Then the problem was completed, and the teacher glanced at the clock and said, 'All right. Now we'll hear the compositions.' He walked to the back of the room, sat down, and then looked around at a field of suddenly upraised hands and said, 'Go ahead, Getsinger. You go first.'

A thin boy with wild blond hair and a red bow tie popped out of his seat and, carrying a sheet of paper, went to the front of the room and, in a fast, singsong voice, read, 'He's So Understanding. I like my Dad because he's so understanding.' Several of the boys turned in their seats and looked at one of the fathers and grinned as Getsinger went on, 'When I ask Dad for a dime he says he'll settle for a nickel, and I say you can't get anything for a nickel any more and he says then he'll settle for six cents. Then pretty soon Mom calls and says that supper is ready, and the fight goes on in the dining room, and after a while Dad says he'll make it seven cents, and before supper is over I have my dime. That's why I say he's understanding.'

Adams smiled in sympathy for Mr Getsinger, and when the next boy got up and started off, 'Why I Like My Father,' Adams realised with horror that all the compositions were going to be on the same subject, and he saw that his own son had a piece of paper on his desk and was waiting eagerly for his turn to read. The palms of Adam's hands became moist, and he looked at the clock, hoping that the time would run out before Bobby got a chance to recite. There was a great deal of laughter during the second boy's reading of his composition, and after he sat down, Adams looked at the clock again and saw that there were seven minutes left. Then the teacher looked around again, and five or six hands shot up, including Bobby's, and the teacher said, 'All right – let's have Satterlee next,' and Bobby took his hand down slowly, and Adams breathed more easily and kept his eyes riveted on the clock.

Satterlee, goaded by the laughter the previous student had received, read his composition with a mincing attempt to be comical, and he told how his father was unable to get any peace around the house, with his mother 'chattering about the latest gossip' and his sister practising the violin. It occurred to Adams that the compositions were nothing more than the children's impressions of their own home life, and the squirming and the nervous laughter from the fathers indicated that the observations were more acute than flattering. Adams tried to think what Bobby might say, and he could remember only things like the time he had docked Bobby's allowance for two weeks, for some offence he couldn't now recall, and the way he sometimes shouted at Bobby when he got too boisterous around the apartment, and the time Bobby had threatened to leave home because he had been forbidden to go to a vaudeville show – and the time he *had* left home because of a punishment Adams had given him. Adams thought also of the night he and his wife had had an argument, and how, the next day, Bobby had asked what 'self-centred' meant, in reply to which Adams had told him it was none of his business. Then he remembered the time Bobby had been on a children's radio show and had announced that his household chores included getting out the ice for drinks, and when Adams asked him later why he had said it, Bobby had reminded him of one time Adams had asked him to bring an ice tray from the pantry into the living room. 'The memories they have,' Adams thought, 'the diabolically selective memories.'

Satterlee finished. The clock showed two minutes to one, and Adams wiped his hands on his trouser legs and gripped his hat, which was getting pulpy around the brim. Then Bobby's hand went up again, almost plaintively now, and the teacher said, 'All right, Adams, you're on,' and Bobby bobbed up and went to the front of the room.

Several of the boys turned and looked at Adams as Bobby began to read, but Adams was oblivious of everything except the stocky figure in front of the blackboard, whose tweed jacket looked too small for him and who was reading fast because the bell was about to ring. What Bobby read was a list of things that Adams had completely forgotten, or that

113

had seemed of no great importance at the time, things like being allowed to stay up late to watch a fight, and being given an old fencing mask when there was no occasion for a gift. (Adams had simply found it in a second-hand store and thought Bobby might like it), and having a model airplane made for him when he couldn't do it himself, and the time Adams had retrieved the ring from the subway grating. By the time Bobby concluded with 'That's why he's OK in *my* book,' Adams had recovered from his surprise and was beginning to feel embarrassed. Then the bell rang and class was dismissed, and Adams and the other fathers followed the boys out of the room.

Bobby was waiting for him in the corridor outside. 'Hi,' Bobby said. 'You going now?'

'Yes,' said Adams. 'I'm afraid I've got to.'

'OK.' Bobby turned and started away.

'Just a minute,' Adams said, and Bobby stopped and looked back. Adams walked over to him and then hesitated a moment. 'That was – ah – a good speech,' he said.

'Thanks,' said Bobby.

Adams started to say something else, but could think of nothing. 'See you later,' he finished, and quickly put on his hat and hurried down the stairs.

Notes for Seize the Fire

Notes for Seize the Fire

Summary
Imagine a world where almost every animal is extinct and the only way of seeing lions, elephants and tigers is by playing virtual reality games. This is how this story begins with Toke, the main character, following a tiger through a virtual tropical jungle. Toke wins a competition to visit one of the few environmental centres where real tigers still live in captivity, but while he is there he uncovers a terrible secret that the centre is trying to hide.

What do you think?
There are some twists and turns in this science fiction story which are quite surprising. They build up a feeling of suspense as, little by little, Toke uncovers an evil organisation pretending to do good. As you read the story, think about:

- how Toke feels when he wins the competition
- the way Toke discovers what the conservation centre is really for
- why Toke becomes involved with Noah's Army
- what could happen to Toke at the end of the story.

Questions
Back up your answers with quotations or references to the story.

1. How is the world of the future described? Explain what has happened to the tigers in the wild at the beginning of this story.

2. What are Toke's first impressions of the Tiger Project Centre? Why does he feel like this?

3. At the centre what does Toke have to do to free Rafi?

4. How is the tiger described when Toke releases him?

Further activity
Design and label your own version of the next conservation centre that Noah's Army plan to free tigers from. Create your own action plan to go with the diagram. Write a list of numbered instructions explaining how the Noah's Army team will free the tigers from this centre.

Seize the Fire

Toke placed his feet as carefully as he could on the forest floor. But, as quiet as each step was on the damp leaves, he knew that his walk was being paced by even softer footfalls. Every now and again he would stop and listen, but all he could hear was the thumping of his own heart and the distant chittering of monkeys and birds.

It was getting dark and soon it would be impossible to see the path without a torch. But it was warm and muggy as only a tropical forest can be. There would be many more hours before the cool of the middle of the night. And then he heard it. One single cough, alarmingly close. He had been right about the silent stalker. The tiger was there.

Toke froze, not daring to lower his foot for the next step. He turned his head slowly towards the direction of the cough. The dying light caught its reflection in two amber eyes in the bushes. A dark shape, brindled with deeper shadows, flowed towards Toke in one easy bound. He felt the hot breath, smelt the tawny tang of big cat and then –

GAME OVER, blinked the message on his goggles.

Toke took off his helmet, sighed and stretched. He had never got any further than this with 'Wild Tiger', sometimes not so far. Most kids played the game because, if you could get to the end of the forest trail before dark without the tiger detecting your presence, you would get an amazing number of credit points on your card – enough to buy your own virtual reality game. Toke played because he wanted to see a tiger.

See it, not smell it or feel its hot breath just before it devoured you. Creep so cautiously that you could circle round behind it and watch it before it saw you. There were over VR programs, of course, the educational ones, but none of them had wild tigers.

And Toke didn't need those programs, not any more. He knew everything there was to know about tigers and had been in love with the big striped cats ever since he was a very small boy. But he had never seen a real one.

In the nineteenth and twentieth centuries there were still tigers all over India and Nepal and Sumatra and Siberia. But by the end of the second millennium there were hardly any left. The rugs and stuffed heads and luxury coats had taken their toll, followed by poachers who sold bones and bits of tiger for medicine and magic.

In 1998 someone had suggested that the problem of tigers in the wild couldn't be solved and that the only way to save tigers was to farm them and kill some of the farmed animals for their body parts. It caused international outrage, but by 2010 it was a fact; the tiger farms began, followed by the elephant and rhino farms.

People were still uneasy about it but the farms were not illegal. At the same time conservation projects took the place of zoos. They were not open to the public but they were devoted to the ideal of looking after large mammals until their natural habitats could be regenerated.

The only zoo Toke had visited was a virtual one, where remaining footage of large mammals was supplemented by computer enhancement and digital tricks. Toke had stroked a tiger in his virtual zoo, but it didn't satisfy him. Nothing would do that except coming face to face with a real tiger. And that was hard to do in 2030.

A yowling from outside his sleep unit door roused Toke from his thoughts. He got up and opened the door and in walked his own private tiger, Geronimo, the closest thing to a wild cat Toke knew. He scooped her up in his arms and sat on the bed while the cat rubbed her cheek against his, telling him how much she loved him with her low rumbling purr.

Just then Toke's mum burst in, gesturing excitedly at the wall where his computer screen was. 'There's an e-mail for you, Toke,' she said. 'From the Global Animal Conservation Trust.'

Toke held his breath. He had entered a competition to win a trip to India, to visit the Tiger Project Centre. He had written a long essay about the future importance of regenerating wild habitats, using all his knowledge and love of tigers to add force to his arguments. Toke turned on his screen and read the message without taking it in.

'Congratulations,' said Mum, reading over his shoulder. 'You won! You'll see your tiger at last.'

Geronimo didn't like all the rushing round over the next few weeks. Mum had to organise time off from her software firm so that she could go with Toke, and he had to get permission to have a week off school. Bags were packed and unpacked. Just how hot would it be in India?

At last Toke and his mum boarded the hover-shuttle to the airport, leaving Dad with many instructions about feeding and caring for the cat. The supersonic flight took four hours and they stepped out into brilliant sunshine and stifling heat. They were grateful to climb into the air-conditioned shuttle that took them to the Tiger Project Centre.

The buildings, including the guest rooms for visitors, were underground and naturally cool. Toke and his mum had adjoining rooms with a sliding door between them. They had nothing to do that first night except meet their host, Dr Greenstreet, the director of the centre. He was a tall, thin man with glasses and the first person Toke had ever met who knew more about tigers than he did.

As Toke lay in his comfortable bed, he thought, I'm in India; but it was hard to believe. His imagination, fuelled by history video-clips, summoned up a tent, a camp-bed, a mosquito net, and the night sounds of the jungle. But in fact he could hear nothing but the whirr of the controlled temperature and humidity unit.

Next morning Dr Greenstreet took Toke on a tour of the centre, beginning with its substantial research facility. Here scientists worked on stored tiger DNA, artificial insemination, diet, diseases and anything else that could affect captive tigers. When Toke thought he couldn't take another laboratory, he was led up a spiral staircase out into the natural light. The sunshine made him blink and his heart was beating fast. He was going to see his first tiger.

It was the smell which reached him first. Not just the musky big-cat smell, familiar from countless virtual reality programs, but the smell of the natural outside world, which he rarely met. The sun beat down on the compound and the trees around it were full of brightly coloured birds and rustlings of small mammals.

Dr Greenstreet took Toke down a shady corridor roofed with plaited bamboo.

'How many tigers are there?' asked Toke.

'About thirty adults and half a dozen cubs at any one time. They are all kept very healthy, because of their regulated diet and our vaccination programme. They're in much better shape than they would be in the wild.'

'But you will return them to the wild as soon as you can, won't you?' asked Toke.

For a moment he thought Dr Greenstreet was going to say no; he seemed to prefer having tigers where he could keep an eye on them. But he quickly smiled and said, 'Of course. But it will take a long time for regeneration to be complete. So much jungle was cleared for agriculture in the late twentieth century.'

Dr Greenstreet punched a code into a computerised door lock at the end of the corridor.

Another worker behind them had been listening. She smiled at Toke. She was a young woman with short curly red hair and freckles. 'But it will happen, Peter,' she said to Dr Greenstreet.

'Ah, Halley,' he said, 'I didn't see you. Will you take over and show our guest the animals? I really should get back to the lab.'

'Sure,' said Halley, taking Toke through the heavy door.

When they were on the other side, she looked at him for a long time before asking, 'What do you think of the centre so far?'

'It makes me want to puke!' said Toke, and then turned bright red, surprised by his own reaction. But he couldn't stop. 'OK, the tigers are well looked after, I guess. And they might be extinct in the wild if you didn't have places like this. But how can you love tigers and be happy to keep them in cages and runs instead of working flat out to get them back into the wild?'

'You do love tigers, don't you?' said Halley softly. She put her hand on Toke's shoulder. 'Come and see them before you say any more.'

She led Toke, still trembling from his outburst, down a metal-lined corridor with bolted doors on either side and then back out into the bright sunshine. And there they were.

Pacing up and down in their separate metal-fenced runs, the big cats swung their tails and shook their heads. Their glossy coats shone and their white teeth flashed as they snarled with every turn. Halley took Toke slowly along the runs, naming all the tigers: Sheba, Solomon, Tariq, Taahra, Yasmin and her cubs, Rafi the two-year-old.

Rafi was a magnificent specimen, a great advertisement for the centre's health claims. As he reached the bars nearest to Toke, he shook his head and made a snuffling noise, a cross between a sneeze and a grunt.

Halley looked quickly both ways to check that there was no-one else in the compound and led Toke to the middle, away from the fences. 'Look,' she said under her breath, 'I shouldn't tell you this, but everything isn't quite what it seems at this centre. I can't talk freely. There are bugs on the gates and CCTV cameras filming everything. Pretend I'm pointing out the security devices to you. Have you been to the computer suite yet?'

'I'm going to get a tour this afternoon,' said Toke, mystified.

'It's a slim chance they'll leave you on your own, but try to find a file called "Investments".'

'What does that mean?' asked Toke. It didn't sound very exciting.

'You'll see,' said Halley grimly. 'Use the password "Farmer". Have you got something you could download the file onto?'

'Yes,' said Toke. 'I've got my pocketbook.'

'Good,' said Halley. 'That'll be very useful to us.'

'Who's "us"?'

'I can't tell you more now, but I'll meet you in the VR room after dinner.'

Just then another worker with a clipboard came out into the compound and pressed a series of buttons which released the calorie-controlled vitamin-enriched tiger food into the animals' feeding areas. Toke went back into the metal corridor and through the security door into the bamboo one.

It was a relief to find his mother waiting for him on the other side. But they were taken to lunch by the director and Toke couldn't tell her everything about his morning. He ate his lunch almost in silence, but his mother was enthusiastic enough for both of them. 'I've been talking to your head of Information Services,' she said. 'I think we could provide you with some software to speed up your data exchange with other centres.'

The computer suite was next to the labs. A white-coated

programmer showed Toke around, demonstrating the state-of-the-art hardware and software. All the tiger projects around the world used a high-speed link to communicate to one another and data was shared once it had been collected. But Toke's mother was sure she could cut seconds off the transfer and was deep in discussion with one of the researchers.

'Choose a tiger,' said Toke's programmer; 'one of the ones you saw this morning.'

'Rafi,' said Toke quickly.

R-A-F-I, typed the programmer. 'There we are!'

The tiger's face filled the screen, every stripe and whisker in sharp definition.

'You can access his height and weight at any date in his history, plus his blood type, DNA structure, his diet, his vaccinations, anything you want to know,' said the programmer, 'and so can any of our colleagues at the other centres.'

He let Toke scroll and click his way through all the data. At the bottom was a box he didn't understand – FORECAST. He clicked on it. The screen bore a single date – 12 June – tomorrow.

'What does that mean?' asked Toke.

The programmer looked at him anxiously. 'You don't need to worry about that. Why don't you look up our records on cubs?'

Just then something started beeping on the lapel of his white coat. 'Excuse me a moment.' He took out a communicator and engaged in a brief conversation. 'Would you mind if I left you on your own for a few minutes? You seem to have picked up the basics. You can carry on looking things up while I'm away.'

Toke put on his politest smile and said he'd be fine. He couldn't believe his luck. FIND FILE. INVESTMENTS, he typed. CLASSIFIED. TOP SECURITY, read the screen; ENTER PASSWORD. FARMER, typed in Toke and was greeted with the message ACCESS GRANTED. As the screen filled up with data on animals and a list of dates, Toke's blood ran cold. There were columns with entries like 'tailbone', 'ribs' and 'skin', with large sums of money beside them. This wasn't a conservation centre at all. It was a cover-up for a tiger farm!

At the bottom of the list was tomorrow's date and the name RAFI. Toke couldn't believe it. Rafi would be killed tomorrow and his beautiful body cut up and sold for profit. Whose profit? Dr Greenstreet's probably. Toke wondered how many other workers at the centre knew about it – Halley, obviously, but she clearly wasn't on Greenstreet's side. Perhaps she could do something to save Rafi?

Toke hastily got out his pocketbook and began to transfer the data. He had just finished and changed the open file by the time the programmer returned. 'I hope you don't mind,' he said. 'I copied some data to use when I write up my report for school.'

The programmer looked at the screen: CARNIVORE DIET, FELID FORMULA. 'That's fine, Toke,' he said.

Halley was waiting for him in the VR room. 'Did you find it?' she whispered.

Toke nodded. 'It's in my pocketbook,' he said. 'Is it safe to talk?'

'Put on this helmet and goggles. If we stand at these two consoles, the CCTV cameras won't know we aren't playing and our intelligence says this room isn't bugged.'

'Who's "us"?' Toke asked for the second time and got a full answer.

It was the weirdest experience of his life, standing next to Halley in a VR helmet listening to her soft voice pour out a crazy story of greed and corruption in high places and an underground movement dedicated to sabotage and the liberation of tigers.

'Noah's Army, that's what we're called. We've liberated twenty tigers from farms, including this so-called conservation project, in the last eighteen months. We can't save them all, of course, or we'd give ourselves away. It has to look like an accident every time.'

'What happens to them afterwards?' asked Toke.

'Eight were shot,' said Halley. 'It's a risk every time. But some of us work outside the farms. We're trying to re-establish the tigers in the wild and to breed enough to make these obscene farms obsolete.'

'Is there anywhere safe for them to live?' asked Toke.

'Yes, one of the regeneration projects is only a few miles from here and the director is sympathetic to Noah's Army. Her own brother is one of our agents.'

'But isn't what you do very dangerous?'

'Incredibly,' said Halley, and Toke could hear she was

grinning. 'We are all crazy, what with the risks of being caught in the farms, and the risks of handling tigers on our own. Of course, the operation here is pretty unusual. We usually liberate tigers from the known farms.'

'Can't you tell someone about Greenstreet and stop him?'

'We were working on that. It was my job to get the data off that "Investments" file, so that we had proof. Thanks to you, we've got that now. But the news about Rafi changes everything. There's no time to get the information to the proper authorities in time to save him. We'll have to carry out an emergency rescue.'

'How?'

Halley didn't answer straight away. Instead she said, 'Toke, have you wondered why I'm telling you all this?'

Toke felt the hairs on his neck rise as he realised he knew the answer. 'You want me to help.'

'One of our key members is sick with a fever. There's no time to get anyone else infiltrated and there's no one I can trust in the centre. It'll take two of us on the inside and at least three on the outside to spring a tiger. It's a lot to ask, but will you step in and help me liberate Rafi?'

'Why me?' asked Toke.

'I think you know,' said Halley. 'It's only people who really love tigers who can be part of Noah's Army.'

It was what Toke wanted to hear but he still couldn't believe it. His brain was in a whirl but there was no time to think it over. 'When?' he whispered.

'Tonight,' said Halley. 'Two o'clock. Here's what we'll do.'

Toke's mother was sure he was coming down with something. 'You've hardly said a word all day and I thought you'd be just buzzing with all those tigers you've seen and everything you've found out.' She insisted on giving him a mediscan and was almost disappointed to discover that his temperature and blood pressure were normal.

'It's OK, Mum,' said Toke. 'I think I'm just tired. You know, it's been a lot to take in. I think I'll get an early night.'

That is a line which always works with mums. She yawned in sympathy. 'Good idea. I think I'll do the same. Being on holiday is so tiring.'

Toke smiled. Mum put in sixteen-hour days at home running her own software business, and she was entitled to a holiday. But instead of sightseeing, she had spent the whole day talking computers with the staff at the centre; she was exhausted: convenient for Toke's first mission with Noah's Army.

At first he thought he'd never do more than doze. But the computer beeped him into wakefulness from a deep sleep. It was one thirty in the morning. He slipped on his shoes and quietly opened his door. The corridor was empty, but shone with a dim green light. Toke found his way to the spiral staircase and crept up and out into the cold night air.

He shivered as he walked down the bamboo corridor, wishing he was wearing something warmer than T-shirt and shorts. When he punched in the code Halley had given him, each beep sounded eerily loud. He slipped through the metal door and froze as a hand grabbed his arm. 'Halley?' he hissed. 'You nearly gave me a heart attack!'

'Sorry,' whispered Halley. 'You got here earlier than I thought you would. The perimeter guards are just passing.'

They waited about three minutes, then slipped out into the compound. The moonlight shone on several tigers, turning their gold bars to silver.

'The farmed tigers are often restless the night before a cull,' whispered Halley. 'We think they sense it.'

'You've done this yourself before?' asked Toke.

'Once or twice,' grinned Halley. 'I've been an inside agent on two farms but this is the first tiger I've liberated from this centre. And I had to get the team together so fast I'm not sure if I've covered all my tracks. So I'm out of here as soon as Rafi is safe.'

Rafi was awake. He lifted his head at their approach and sniffed the air. Then he came up to the bars of his run and made the snuffle of greeting.

'Don't worry, Rafi,' Toke told him. 'We're going to get you out.'

'Remember what I told you, Toke,' warned Halley. 'He's still a big dangerous meat-eater, not a pussycat. Never stop being afraid, or you could make a serious mistake.'

Toke heard a low whistle from the outer fence and knew that there were other members of Noah's Army out there. It made him feel braver than he really was. But there was no disguising that this was the most dangerous thing he had ever done. And, unlike the others, he was only a kid.

The next few moments were crucial. Halley had organised a 'power failure', which would immobilise the cameras, microphones and alarm system for about ten minutes. She was going to open Rafi's door and the gate in the perimeter fence. She knew the combinations, of course, but had to make it look as if it were linked to the fluctuation in the power supply. The outside team was going to accept Rafi as soon as he was out. But getting the tiger out was a two-person job, which was where Toke came in.

'Ready?' asked Halley.

Toke nodded.

She punched the combination into the lock on Rafi's cage and released the door, then held it in place. Rafi was just on the other side.

'Quick, hold the door while I release the gate,' said Halley.

Toke put his weight against the door, wedging it almost but not quite shut. He looked into Rafi's eyes while Halley dealt with the outer gate. Then they swapped places, with Toke holding the outside gate, while Halley prepared to release the tiger.

She nodded to Toke in the moonlight. He whistled softly twice to the waiting team, to signal that the time had come. Then he opened the gate outwards into the jungle. A split second later Halley opened Rafi's door and called him out.

The tiger moved cautiously out of his run. The outside team had brought meat with them to lure him towards the gate and he caught the aroma. Slowly he paced across the compound to the outer fence, ignoring Halley, who had closed in behind him to block his retreat.

Toke held his breath. The huge head lifted and Rafi looked him in the eyes once more. Then the sinuous black and gold body slipped past him and out of the gate, so close that the tiger's fur brushed his bare legs. Rafi had escaped.

But in that moment of triumph, Toke's exultation turned to terror as he heard the sound of people in the metal corridor.

Halley froze for a second, then did the unthinkable. She thrust Toke out into the night. 'Hide!' she hissed.

There was no time for further explanation. Toke hid.

From behind the bushes outside the compound he could hear voices – several male voices – raised in anger, then Halley's, calm and explanatory. Suddenly an ear-piercing alarm went off and bright searchlights flashed on all along the perimeter fence. Toke had to move fast. Guards were rushing to the gate from both inside and outside the fence. Toke turned and ran.

He ran until he had a stitch, then stopped, doubled up, to get his breath back. The shouts from the centre had faded and he was deep in the heart of the jungle. He had no idea where he was. And then suddenly he recognised it.

He was on a path just like the one in 'Wild Tiger'. He inched his way soundlessly along, sure that another, softer footfall was matching him pace for pace. Was it Rafi? Halley had told him that another tiger liberated from this centre, Rukhshana, was living in the regenerated habitat nearby. They hoped that Rafi would mate with her and that she would bring two or three cubs to adulthood in the wild. Suppose Rukhshana had wandered close to the centre? If his silent companion was the tigress, she wouldn't know him. Did a love of tigers show in the dark? Toke wondered.

Then he heard a tiger cough. Oh God, I know how the next bit goes, thought Toke, expecting the rush of air, the hot stinking breath and then extinction. Only this time it would be for real.

But it wasn't 'Wild Tiger'. The tiger came towards him down the path and, after a few seconds of sheer terror, Toke saw that it was Rafi and that he had a large piece of raw meat in his jaws. Behind him came three people in camouflage fatigues, two men and a woman.

The people stopped in their tracks but Rafi came on. As he approached Toke, he paused and gave his snuffling grunt, muffled by the meat. Toke grunted back and the members of Noah's Army relaxed. 'You must be Toke,' said one of the men. 'What happened back there? Is Halley OK?'

'I don't know,' said Toke. 'Some people came into the tiger compound and she shoved me out of the gate. I heard them talking to her but then all hell broke loose and I just ran.'

There was a quick consultation, then the man said, 'I'll take you back and get you into the centre. Then I'll see if I can get Halley out. The others can look after Rafi till we rejoin them.'

They crept back through the jungle, Keti, as he was called, leading Toke round to the other side of the centre. There were no guards at the front; all their attention was directed to where animals might get out, not people in. Keti knew the security overrides and soon opened the door to the sleeping quarters.

'Go carefully, Toke,' he whispered. 'And well done. You've made a great start in the Army, releasing your first tiger. You're our youngest member ever. We'll be in touch.'

'See you,' said Toke. He stood for a while in the corridor, adjusting his eyes to the green light. He was bracing himself to get back into his room, hoping that the alarms hadn't wakened his mother. Bracing himself, too, for whatever had happened to Halley.

But whatever happened, he was now a member of Noah's Army. He had released his first tiger. And of one thing he was sure: it was not going to be the last.

Notes for Rats

Summary

The setting of this ghost story creates an eerie atmosphere. An innocent traveller stops at a countryside inn with a mysterious locked room. The author, M. R. James, builds up a picture of an ordinary holiday, which he undercuts with strange details giving the reader an unsettling feeling.

What do you think?

The strength of this story is the atmosphere that M. R. James creates using detailed descriptions of the characters, landscape and buildings. As you read, think about the following:

- How are the landscape and buildings described? What effect do these have on you as a reader?
- How is Mr Thompson described? What do you think of him?
- Do you believe the landlord's explanation of the strange activities?

Questions

Choose words and phrases from the story to back up your answers.

1. What do you think the first paragraph describes?
2. What is the first mysterious thing that Mr Thompson notices? Explain why this is important later on in the story.
3. How is the landlord's accent different from your accent? Pick out examples of things that he says that show this.
4. How does the author build up tension when Mr Thompson discovers the room with the 'scarecrow'?
5. How is the 'scarecrow' described? Why does the author use questions in this section?

Further activity

'…what he may do now there ain't no sayin'.' So the landlord says after Mr Thompson has disturbed the ghost. Imagine the ghost does come back. Storyboard what happens next as though you are adapting this new story as a film. Use some of the following techniques:

- Create an effective beginning. This could be a false sense of security or a sense of fear.
- Think about descriptions of landscape and buildings.
- Build up to a dramatic ending.

Rats

'And if you was to walk through the bedrooms now, you'd see the ragged, mouldy bedclothes a-heaving and a-heaving like seas.' 'And a-heaving and a-heaving with what?' he says. 'Why, with the rats under 'em.'

But was it with the rats? I ask, because in another case it was not. I cannot put a date to the story, but I was young when I heard it, and the teller was old. It is an ill-proportioned tale, but that is my fault, not his.

It happened in Suffolk, near the coast. In a place where the road makes a sudden dip and then a sudden rise; as you go northward, at the top of that rise, stands a house on the left of the road. It is a tall red-brick house, narrow for its height; perhaps it was built about 1770. The top of the front has a low triangular pediment with a round window in the centre. Behind it are stables and offices, and such garden as it has is behind them. Scraggy Scotch firs are near it: an expanse of gorse-covered land stretches away from it. It commands a view of the distant sea from the upper windows of the front. A sign on a post stands before the door; or did so stand, for though it was an inn of repute once, I believe it is so no longer.

To this inn came my acquaintance, Mr Thomson, when he was a young man, on a fine spring day, coming from the University of Cambridge, and desirous of solitude in tolerable quarters and time for reading. These he found, for the landlord and his wife had been in service and could make a visitor comfortable, and there was no one else staying in the inn. He had a large room on the first floor commanding the road and the view, and if it faced east, why, that could not be helped; the house was well built and warm.

He spent very tranquil and uneventful days: work all the morning, an afternoon perambulation of the country round, a little conversation with country company or the people of the inn in the evening over the then fashionable drink of brandy and water, a little more reading and writing, and bed; and he would have been content that this should continue for the full month he had at disposal, so well was his work progressing, and so fine was the April of that year – which I have reason to believe was that which Orlando Whistlecraft chronicles in his weather record as the 'Charming Year.'

One of his walks took him along the northern road, which stands high and traverses a wide common, called a heath. On the bright afternoon when he first chose this direction his eye caught a white object some hundreds of yards to the left of the road, and he felt it necessary to make sure what this might be. It was not long before he was standing by it, and found himself looking at a square block of white stone fashioned somewhat like the base of a pillar, with a square hole in the upper surface. Just such another you may see at this day on Thetford Heath. After taking stock of it he contemplated for a few minutes the view, which offered a church tower or two, some red roofs of cottages and windows winking in the sun, and the expanse of sea also with an occasional wink and gleam upon it – and so pursued his way.

In the desultory evening talk in the bar, he asked why the white stone was there on the common.

'A old-fashioned thing, that is,' said the landlord (Mr Betts), 'we was none of us alive when that was put there.' 'That's right,' said another. 'It stands pretty high,' said Mr Thomson, 'I dare say a sea-mark was on it some time back.' 'Ah! yes,' Mr Betts agreed, 'I 'ave 'eard they could see it from the boats; but whatever there was, it's fell to bits this long time.' 'Good job too,' said a third, ''twarn't a lucky mark, by what the old men used to say; not lucky for the fishin', I mean to say.' 'Why ever not?' said Thomson. 'Well, I never see it myself,' was the answer, 'but they 'ad some funny ideas, what I mean, peculiar, them old chaps, and I shouldn't wonder but what they made away with it theirselves.'

It was impossible to get anything clearer than this: the company, never very voluble, fell silent, and when next someone spoke it was of village affairs and crops. Mr Betts was the speaker.

Not every day did Thomson consult his health by taking a country walk. One very fine afternoon found him busily writing at three o'clock. Then he stretched himself and rose, and walked out of his room into the passage. Facing him was another room, then the stairhead, then two more rooms, one looking out to the back, the other to the south. At the south end of the passage was a window, to which he went, considering with himself that it was rather a shame to waste such a fine afternoon. However, work was paramount just at the moment; he thought he would just take five minutes off and go back to it; and those five minutes he would employ – the Bettses could

137

not possibly object – to looking at the other rooms in the passage, which he had never seen. Nobody at all, it seemed, was indoors; probably, as it was market day, they were all gone to the town, except perhaps a maid in the bar. Very still the house was, and the sun shone really hot; early flies buzzed in the window-panes. So he explored. The room facing his own was undistinguished except for an old print of Bury St Edmunds; the two next to him on his side of the passage were gay and clean, with one window apiece, whereas his had two. Remained the south-west room, opposite to the last which he had entered. This was locked; but Thomson was in a mood of quite indefensible curiosity, and feeling confident that there could be no damaging secrets in a place so easily got at, he proceeded to fetch the key of his own room, and when that did not answer, to collect the keys of the other three. One of them fitted, and he opened the door. The room had two windows looking south and west, so it was as bright and the sun as hot upon it as could be. Here there was no carpet, but bare boards; no pictures, no washing-stand, only a bed, in the farther corner: an iron bed, with mattress and bolster, covered with a bluish check counterpane. As featureless a room as you can well imagine, and yet there was something that made Thomson close the door very quickly and yet quietly behind him and lean against the window-sill in the passage, actually quivering all over. It was this, that under the counterpane someone lay, and not only lay, but stirred. That it was some *one* and not some *thing* was certain, because the shape of a head was unmistakable on the bolster; and yet it was all covered, and no one lies with covered head but a dead person;

and this was not dead, not truly dead, for it heaved and shivered. If he had seen these things in dusk or by the light of a flickering candle, Thomson could have comforted himself and talked of fancy. On this bright day that was impossible. What was to be done? First, lock the door at all costs. Very gingerly he approached it and bending down listened, holding his breath; perhaps there might be a sound of heavy breathing, and a prosaic explanation. There was absolute silence. But as, with a rather tremulous hand, he put the key into its hole and turned it, it rattled, and on the instant a stumbling padding tread was heard coming towards the door. Thomson fled like a rabbit to his room and locked himself in: futile enough, he knew it was; would doors and locks be any obstacle to what he suspected? But it was all he could think of at the moment, and in fact nothing happened; only there was a time of acute suspense – followed by a misery of doubt as to what to do. The impulse, of course, was to slip away as soon as possible from a house which contained such an inmate. But only the day before he had said he should be staying for at least a week more, and how if he changed plans could he avoid the suspicion of having pried into places where he certainly had no business? Moreover, either the Bettses knew all about the inmate, and yet did not leave the house, or knew nothing, which equally meant that there was nothing to be afraid of, or knew just enough to make them shut up the room, but not enough to weigh on their spirits: in any of these cases it seemed that not much was to be feared, and certainly so far he had had no sort of ugly experience. On the whole the line of least resistance was to stay.

139

Well, he stayed out his week. Nothing took him past that door, and, often as he would pause in a quiet hour of day or night in the passage and listen, and listen, no sound whatever issued from that direction. You might have thought that Thomson would have made some attempt at ferreting out stories connected with the inn – hardly perhaps from Betts, but from the parson of the parish, or old people in the village; but no, the reticence which commonly falls on people who have had strange experiences, and believe in them, was upon him. Nevertheless, as the end of his stay drew near, his yearning after some kind of explanation grew more and more acute. On his solitary walks he persisted in planning out some way, the least obtrusive, of getting another daylight glimpse into that room, and eventually arrived at this scheme. He would leave by an afternoon train – about four o'clock. When his fly was waiting, and his luggage on it, he would make one last expedition upstairs to look round his own room and see if anything was left unpacked, and then, with that key, which he had contrived to oil (as if that made any difference!), the door should once more be opened, for a moment, and shut.

So it worked out. The bill was paid, the consequent small talk gone through while the fly was loaded: 'pleasant part of the country – been very comfortable, thanks to you and Mrs Betts – hope to come back some time,' on one side: on the other, 'very glad you've found satisfaction, sir, done our best – always glad to 'ave your good word – very much favoured we've been with the weather, to be sure.' Then, 'I'll just take a look upstairs in case I've left a book or something out – no, don't trouble, I'll be back in a minute.' And as noiselessly as possible he stole to the door and opened it. The shattering of the illusion! He almost laughed aloud. Propped, or you might say sitting, on the edge of the bed was – nothing in the round world but a scarecrow! A scarecrow out of the garden, of course, dumped into the deserted room ... Yes; but here amusement ceased. Have scarecrows bare bony feet? Do their heads loll on to their shoulders? Have they iron collars and links of chain about their necks? Can they get up and move, if ever so stiffly, across a floor, with wagging head and arms close at their sides? and shiver?

The slam of the door, the dash to the stair-head, the leap downstairs, were followed by a faint. Awaking, Thomson saw Betts standing over him with the brandy bottle and a very reproachful face. 'You shouldn't a done so, sir, really you shouldn't. It ain't a kind way to act by persons as done the best they could for you.' Thomson heard words of this kind, but what he said in reply he did not know. Mr Betts, and perhaps even more Mrs Betts, found it hard to accept his apologies and his assurances that he would say no word that could damage the good name of the house. However, they *were* accepted. Since the train could not now be caught, it was arranged that Thomson should be driven to the town to sleep there. Before he went the Bettses told him what little they knew, 'They says he was landlord 'ere a long time back, and was in with the 'ighwaymen that 'ad their beat about the 'eath. That's how he come by his end: 'ung in chains, they say, up where you see that stone what the gallus stood in. Yes, the fishermen made away with that, I believe, because they see it out at sea and it kep' the fish off, according to their idea. Yes, we 'ad the account from the people that 'ad the 'ouse before we come. "You keep that room shut up," they says, "but don't move the bed out, and you'll find there won't be no trouble." And no more there 'as been; not once he haven't come out into the 'ouse, though what he may do now there ain't no sayin'. Anyway, you're the first I know on that's seen him since we've been 'ere: I never set eyes on him myself, nor don't want. And ever since we've made the servants' rooms in the stablin', we ain't 'ad no difficulty that way. Only I do 'ope, sir, as you'll keep a close tongue, considerin' 'ow an 'ouse do get talked about': with more to this effect.

The promise of silence was kept for many years. The occasion of my hearing the story at last was this: that when Mr Thomson came to stay with my father it fell to me to show him to his room, and instead of letting me open the door for him, he stepped forward and threw it open himself, and then for some moments stood in the doorway holding up his candle and looking narrowly into the interior. Then he seemed to recollect himself and said: 'I beg your pardon. Very absurd, but I can't help doing that, for a particular reason.' What that reason was I heard some days afterwards, and you have heard now.

Notes for The Speckled Band

Summary

In this story Sherlock Holmes solves one murder while preventing another one from happening, and all this time Doctor Watson has not got a clue about what is going on. Right from the beginning of the story, Sherlock Holmes is piecing clues together. The strength of the story is when seemingly meaningless details are put together to find a murderer.

What do you think?

This story was written over a hundred years ago and so it contains quite a lot of old-fashioned language. However the structure of the story is quite simple: first Doctor Watson, the narrator of the story, sets the scene. Then Sherlock Holmes interviews a distressed lady visitor who explains her problem. Finally Sherlock Holmes and Doctor Watson go to the village where the lady lives and solve the mystery. While you read the story think about:

- the details that Helen Stoner tells Sherlock Holmes when describing what happened to her sister
- why Doctor Roylott visits Sherlock Holmes
- your own ideas about what has happened.

Questions

Back up your answers with quotations or references to the story.

1. Which case prompted Helen Stoner to visit Sherlock Holmes?

2. How does Sherlock Holmes work out how Helen has travelled to see him?

3. Explain the past history of Helen, her family and Doctor Roylott.

4. Describe how Helen's sister dies. What do you think she has died of?

5. Read up to the section that describes Helen's room. You now have all the information that Sherlock Holmes has. Now, decide:

a) What is the speckled band?

b) How did Helen's sister die?

c) What is going on in the house now?

Further activity

Write your own mystery story. Structure the story in the following way:

- Set the scene.
- Introduce and interview the main characters.
- Describe the investigation and explain how the mystery is solved.

The Speckled Band

On glancing over my notes of the seventy odd cases in which I have during the last eight years studied the methods of my friend Sherlock Holmes, I find many tragic, some comic, a large number merely strange, but none commonplace; for, working as he did rather for the love of his art than for the acquirement of wealth, he refused to associate himself with any investigation which did not tend towards the unusual, and even the fantastic. Of all these varied cases, however, I cannot recall any which presented more singular features than that which was associated with the well-known Surrey family of the Roylotts of Stoke Moran. The events in question occurred in the early days of my association with Holmes, when we were sharing rooms as bachelors in Baker Street. It is possible that I might have placed them upon record before, but a promise of secrecy was made at the time, from which I have only been freed during the last month by the untimely death of the lady to whom the pledge was given. It is perhaps as well that the facts should now come to light, for I have reasons to know that there are widespread rumours as to the death of Dr Grimesby Roylott which tend to make the matter even more terrible than the truth.

It was early in April in the year '83 that I woke one morning to find Sherlock Holmes standing, fully dressed, by the side of my bed. He was a late riser, as a rule, and as the clock on the mantelpiece showed me that it was only a quarter-past seven, I blinked up at him in some surprise, and perhaps just a little resentment, for I was myself regular in my habits.

'Very sorry to knock you up, Watson,' said he, 'but it's the common lot this morning. Mrs Hudson has been knocked up, she retorted upon me, and I on you.'

'What is it, then – a fire?'

'No; a client. It seems that a young lady has arrived in a considerable state of excitement, who insists upon seeing me. She is waiting now in the sitting-room. Now, when young ladies wander about the metropolis at this hour of the morning, and knock sleepy people up out of their beds, I presume that it is something very pressing which they have to communicate. Should it prove to be an interesting case, you would, I am sure, wish to follow it from the outset. I thought, at any rate, that I should call you and give you the chance.'

'My dear fellow, I would not miss it for anything.'

I had no keener pleasure than in following Holmes in his professional investigations, and in admiring the rapid deductions, as swift as intuitions, and yet always founded on a logical basis with which he unravelled the problems which were submitted to him. I rapidly threw on my clothes and was ready in a few minutes to accompany my friend down to the sitting-room. A lady dressed in black and heavily veiled, who had been sitting in the window, rose as we entered.

'Good-morning, madam,' said Holmes cheerily. 'My name is Sherlock Holmes. This is my intimate friend and associate, Dr Watson, before whom you can speak as freely as before myself. Ha! I am glad to see that Mrs Hudson has had the good sense to light the fire. Pray draw up to it, and I shall order you a cup of hot coffee, for I observe that you are shivering.'

'It is not cold which makes me shiver,' said the woman in a low voice, changing her seat as requested.

'What, then?'

'It is fear, Mr Holmes. It is terror.' She raised her veil as she spoke, and we could see that she was indeed in a pitiable state of agitation, her face all drawn and grey, with restless frightened eyes, like those of some hunted animal. Her features and figure were those of a woman of thirty, but her hair was shot with premature grey, and her expression was weary and haggard. Sherlock Holmes ran her over with one of his quick, all-comprehensive glances.

'You must not fear,' said he soothingly, bending forward and patting her forearm. 'We shall soon set matters right, I have no doubt. You have come in by train this morning, I see.'

'You know me, then?'

'No, but I observe the second half of a return ticket in the palm of your left glove. You must have started early, and yet you had a good drive in a dog-cart, along heavy roads, before you reached the station.'

The lady gave a violent start and stared in bewilderment at my companion.

'There is no mystery, my dear madam,' said he, smiling. 'The left arm of your jacket is spattered with mud in no less than seven places. The marks are perfectly fresh. There is no vehicle save a dog-cart which throws up mud in that way, and then only when you sit on the left-hand side of the driver.'

'Whatever your reasons may be, you are perfectly correct,' said she. 'I started from home before six, reached Leatherhead at twenty past, and came in by the first train to Waterloo. Sir,

I can stand this strain no longer; I shall go mad if it continues. I have no one to turn to – none, save only one, who cares for me, and he, poor fellow, can be of little aid. I have heard of you, Mr Holmes; I have heard of you from Mrs Farintosh, whom you helped in the hour of her sore need. It was from her that I had your address. Oh, sir, do you not think that you could help me, too, and at least throw a little light through the dense darkness which surrounds me? At present it is out of my power to reward you for your services, but in a month or six weeks I shall be married, with the control of my own income, and then at least you shall not find me ungrateful.'

Holmes turned to his desk and, unlocking it, drew out a small case-book, which he consulted.

'Farintosh,' said he. 'Ah yes, I recall the case; it was concerned with an opal tiara. I think it was before your time, Watson. I can only say, madam, that I shall be happy to devote the same care to your case as I did to that of your friend. As to reward, my profession is its own reward; but you are at liberty to defray whatever expenses I may be put to, at the time which suits you best. And now I beg that you will lay before us everything that may help us in forming an opinion upon the matter.'

'Alas!' replied our visitor, 'the very horror of my situation lies in the fact that my fears are so vague, and my suspicions depend so entirely upon small points, which might seem trivial to another, that even he to whom of all others I have a right to look for help and advice looks upon all that I tell him about it as the fancies of a nervous woman. He does not say so, but I can read it from his soothing answers and averted eyes. But I have heard, Mr Holmes, that you can see deeply into the

148

manifold wickedness of the human heart. You may advise me how to walk amid the dangers which encompass me.'

'I am all attention, madam.'

'My name is Helen Stoner, and I am living with my stepfather, who is the last survivor of one of the oldest Saxon families in England, the Roylotts of Stoke Moran, on the western border of Surrey.'

Holmes nodded his head. 'The name is familiar to me,' said he.

'The family was at one time among the richest in England, and the estates extended over the borders into Berkshire in the north, and Hampshire in the west. In the last century, however, four successive heirs were of a dissolute and wasteful disposition, and the family ruin was eventually completed by a gambler in the days of the Regency. Nothing was left save a few acres of ground, and the two-hundred-year-old house, which is itself crushed under a heavy mortgage. The last squire dragged out his existence there, living the horrible life of an aristocratic pauper; but his only son, my stepfather, seeing that he must adapt himself to the new conditions, obtained an advance from a relative, which enabled him to take a medical degree, and went out to Calcutta, where, by his professional skill and his force of character, he established a large practice. In a fit of anger, however, caused by some robberies which had been perpetrated in the house, he beat his native butler to death and narrowly escaped a capital sentence. As it was, he suffered a long term of imprisonment and afterwards returned to England a morose and disappointed man.

'When Dr Roylott was in India he married my mother, Mrs Stoner, the young widow of Major-General Stoner, of the Bengal Artillery. My sister Julia and I were twins, and we were only two years old at the time of my mother's re-marriage. She had a considerable sum of money – not less than 1000 pounds a year – and this she bequeathed to Dr Roylott entirely while we resided with him, with a provision that a certain annual sum should be allowed to each of us in the event of our marriage. Shortly after our return to England my mother died – she was killed eight years ago in a railway accident near Crewe. Dr Roylott then abandoned his attempts to establish himself in practice in London and took us to live with him in the old ancestral house at Stoke Moran. The money which my mother had left was enough for all our wants, and there seemed to be no obstacle to our happiness.

'But a terrible change came over our stepfather about this time. Instead of making friends and exchanging visits with our neighbours, who had at first been overjoyed to see a Roylott of Stoke Moran back in the old family seat, he shut himself up in his house and seldom came out save to indulge in ferocious quarrels with whoever might cross his path. Violence of temper approaching to mania has been hereditary in the men of the family, and in my stepfather's case it had, I believe, been intensified by his long residence in the tropics. A series of disgraceful brawls took place, two of which ended in the police-court, until at last he became the terror of the village, and the folks would fly at his approach, for he is a man of immense strength, and absolutely uncontrollable in his anger.

'Last week he hurled the local blacksmith over a parapet into a stream, and it was only by paying over all the money which I could gather together that I was able to avert another public exposure. He had no friends at all save the wandering gypsies, and he would give these vagabonds leave to encamp upon the few acres of bramble-covered land which represent the family estate, and would accept in return the hospitality of their tents, wandering away with them sometimes for weeks on end. He has a passion also for Indian animals, which are sent over to him by a correspondent, and he has at this moment a cheetah and a baboon, which wander freely over his grounds and are feared by the villagers almost as much as their master.

'You can imagine from what I say that my poor sister Julia and I had no great pleasure in our lives. No servant would stay with us, and for a long time we did all the work of the house. She was but thirty at the time of her death, and yet her hair had already begun to whiten, even as mine has.'

'Your sister is dead, then?'

'She died just two years ago, and it is of her death that I wish to speak to you. You can understand that, living the life which I have described, we were little likely to see anyone of our own age and position. We had, however, an aunt, my mother's maiden sister, Miss Honoria Westphail, who lives near Harrow, and we were occasionally allowed to pay short visits at this lady's house. Julia went there at Christmas two years ago, and met there a half-pay major of marines, to whom she became engaged. My stepfather learned of the engagement when my sister returned and offered no objection to the marriage; but within a fortnight of the day which had been fixed for the wedding, the terrible event occurred which has deprived me of my only companion.'

Sherlock Holmes had been leaning back in his chair with his eyes closed and his head sunk in a cushion, but he half opened his lids now and glanced across at his visitor.

'Pray be precise as to details,' said he.

'It is easy for me to be so, for every event of that dreadful time is seared into my memory. The manor-house is, as I have already said, very old, and only one wing is now inhabited. The bedrooms in this wing are on the ground floor, the sitting-rooms being in the central block of the buildings. Of these bedrooms the first is Dr Roylott's, the second my sister's, and the third my own. There is no communication between them, but they all open out into the same corridor. Do I make myself plain?'

'Perfectly so.'

'The windows of the three rooms open out upon the lawn. That fatal night Dr Roylott had gone to his room early, though we knew that he had not retired to rest, for my sister was troubled by the smell of the strong Indian cigars which it was his custom to smoke. She left her room, therefore, and came into mine, where she sat for some time, chatting about her approaching wedding. At eleven o'clock she rose to leave me, but she paused at the door and looked back.

'"Tell me, Helen," said she, "have you ever heard anyone whistle in the dead of the night?"

'"Never," said I.

'"I suppose that you could not possibly whistle, yourself, in your sleep?"

' "Certainly not. But why?"

' "Because during the last few nights I have always, about three in the morning, heard a low, clear whistle. I am a light sleeper, and it has awakened me. I cannot tell where it came from, perhaps from the next room, perhaps from the lawn. I thought that I would just ask you whether you had heard it."

' "No, I have not. It must be those wretched gypsies in the plantation."

' "Very likely. And yet if it were on the lawn, I wonder that you did not hear it also."

' "Ah, but I sleep more heavily than you."

' "Well, it is of no great consequence, at any rate." She smiled back at me, closed my door, and a few moments later I heard her key turn in the lock.'

'Indeed,' said Holmes. 'Was it your custom always to lock yourselves in at night?'

'Always.'

'And why?'

'I think that I mentioned to you that the doctor kept a cheetah and a baboon. We had no feeling of security unless our doors were locked.'

'Quite so. Pray proceed with your statement.'

'I could not sleep that night. A vague feeling of impending misfortune impressed me. My sister and I, you will recollect, were twins, and you know how subtle are the links which bind two souls which are so closely allied. It was a wild night. The wind was howling outside, and the rain was beating and splashing against the windows. Suddenly, amid all the hubbub of the gale, there burst forth the wild scream of a terrified woman. I knew that it was my sister's voice. I sprang from my bed, wrapped a shawl round me, and rushed into the corridor. As I opened my door I seemed to hear a low whistle, such as my sister described, and a few moments later a clanging sound, as if a mass of metal had fallen. As I ran down the passage, my sister's door was unlocked, and revolved slowly upon its hinges. I stared at it horror-stricken, not knowing what was about to issue from it. By the light of the corridor-lamp I saw my sister appear at the opening, her face blanched with terror, her hands groping for help, her whole figure swaying to and fro like that of a drunkard. I ran to her and threw my arms round her, but at that moment her knees seemed to give way and she fell to the ground. She writhed as one who is in terrible pain, and her limbs were dreadfully convulsed. At first I thought that she had not recognised me, but as I bent over her she suddenly shrieked out in a voice which I shall never forget, "Oh, my God! Helen! It was the band! The speckled band!" There was something else which she would fain have said, and she stabbed with her finger into the air in the direction of the doctor's room, but a fresh convulsion seized her and choked her words. I rushed out, calling loudly for my stepfather, and I met him hastening from his room in his dressing-gown. When he reached my sister's side she was unconscious, and though he poured brandy down her throat and sent for medical aid from the village, all efforts were in vain, for she slowly sank and died without having recovered her consciousness. Such was the dreadful end of my beloved sister.'

'One moment,' said Holmes, 'are you sure about this whistle and metallic sound? Could you swear to it?'

'That was what the county coroner asked me at the inquiry. It is my strong impression that I heard it, and yet, among the crash of the gale and the creaking of an old house, I may possibly have been deceived.'

'Was your sister dressed?'

'No, she was in her night-dress. In her right hand was found the charred stump of a match, and in her left a match-box.'

'Showing that she had struck a light and looked about her when the alarm took place. That is important. And what conclusions did the coroner come to?'

'He investigated the case with great care, for Dr Roylott's conduct had long been notorious in the county, but he was unable to find any satisfactory cause of death. My evidence showed that the door had been fastened upon the inner side, and the windows were blocked by old-fashioned shutters with broad iron bars, which were secured every night. The walls were carefully sounded, and were shown to be quite solid all round, and the flooring was also thoroughly examined, with the same result. The chimney is wide, but is barred up by four large staples. It is certain, therefore, that my sister was quite alone when she met her end. Besides, there were no marks of any violence upon her.'

'How about poison?'

'The doctors examined her for it, but without success.'

'What do you think that this unfortunate lady died of, then?'

'It is my belief that she died of pure fear and nervous shock, though what it was that frightened her I cannot imagine.'

'Were there gypsies in the plantation at the time?'

'Yes, there are nearly always some there.'

'Ah, and what did you gather from this allusion to a band – a speckled band?'

'Sometimes I have thought that it was merely the wild talk of delirium, sometimes that it may have referred to some band of people, perhaps to these very gypsies in the plantation. I do not know whether the spotted handkerchiefs which so many of them wear over their heads might have suggested the strange adjective which she used.'

Holmes shook his head like a man who is far from being satisfied.

'These are very deep waters,' said he; 'pray go on with your narrative.'

'Two years have passed since then, and my life has been until lately lonelier than ever. A month ago, however, a dear friend, whom I have known for many years, has done me the honour to ask my hand in marriage. His name is Armitage – Percy Armitage – the second son of Mr Armitage, of Crane Water, near Reading. My stepfather has offered no opposition to the match, and we are to be married in the course of the spring. Two days ago some repairs were started in the west wing of the building, and my bedroom wall has been pierced, so that I have had to move into the chamber in which my sister died, and to sleep in the very bed in which she slept. Imagine, then, my thrill of terror when last night, as I lay awake, thinking over her terrible fate, I suddenly heard in the silence of the night the low whistle which had been the herald of her own death. I sprang up and lit the lamp, but nothing was to be seen in the room. I was too shaken to go to bed again, however, so I dressed, and as soon as it was daylight I slipped down, got a dog-cart at the Crown Inn, which is opposite, and drove to Leatherhead, from whence I have come on this morning with the one object of seeing you and asking your advice.'

'You have done wisely,' said my friend. 'But have you told me all?'

'Yes, all.'

'Miss Stoner, you have not. You are screening your stepfather.'

'Why, what do you mean?'

For answer Holmes pushed back the frill of black lace which fringed the hand that lay upon our visitor's knee. Five little livid spots, the marks of four fingers and a thumb, were printed upon the white wrist.

'You have been cruelly used,' said Holmes.

The lady coloured deeply and covered over her injured wrist. 'He is a hard man,' she said, 'and perhaps he hardly knows his own strength.'

There was a long silence, during which Holmes leaned his chin upon his hands and stared into the crackling fire.

'This is a very deep business,' he said at last. 'There are a thousand details which I should desire to know before I decide upon our course of action. Yet we have not a moment to lose. If we were to come to Stoke Moran to-day, would it be possible for us to see over these rooms without the knowledge of your stepfather?'

'As it happens, he spoke of coming into town to-day upon some most important business. It is probable that he will be away all day, and that there would be nothing to disturb you. We have a housekeeper now, but she is old and foolish, and I could easily get her out of the way.'

'Excellent. You are not averse to this trip, Watson?'

'By no means.'

'Then we shall both come. What are you going to do yourself?'

'I have one or two things which I would wish to do now that I am in town. But I shall return by the twelve o'clock train, so as to be there in time for your coming.'

'And you may expect us early in the afternoon. I have myself some small business matters to attend to. Will you not wait and breakfast?'

'No, I must go. My heart is lightened already since I have confided my trouble to you. I shall look forward to seeing you again this afternoon.' She dropped her thick black veil over her face and glided from the room.

'And what do you think of it all, Watson?' asked Sherlock Holmes, leaning back in his chair.

'It seems to me to be a most dark and sinister business.'

'Dark enough and sinister enough.'

'Yet if the lady is correct in saying that the flooring and walls are sound, and that the door, window and chimney are impassable, then her sister must have been undoubtedly alone when she met her mysterious end.'

'What becomes, then, of these noctural whistles, and what of the very peculiar words of the dying woman?'

'I cannot think.'

'When you combine the ideas of whistles at night, the presence of a band of gypsies who are on intimate terms with this old doctor, the fact that we have every reason to believe that the doctor has an interest in preventing his stepdaughter's marriage, the dying allusion to a band, and, finally, the fact that Miss Helen Stoner heard a metallic clang, which might have been caused by one of those metal bars that secured the shutters falling back into its place, I think that there is good ground to think that the mystery may be cleared along those lines.'

'But what, then, did the gypsies do?'

'I cannot imagine.'

'I see many objections to any such theory.'

'And so do I. It is precisely for that reason that we are going to Stoke Moran this day. I want to see whether the objections are fatal, or if they may be explained away. But what in the name of the devil!'

The ejaculation had been drawn from my companion by the fact that our door had been suddenly dashed open, and that a huge man had framed himself in the aperture. His costume was a peculiar mixture of the professional and of the agricultural, having a black top-hat, a long frock-coat and a pair of high gaiters, with a hunting-crop swinging in his hand. So tall was he that his hat actually brushed the cross bar of the doorway, and his breadth seemed to span it across from side to side. A large face, seared with a thousand wrinkles, burned yellow with the sun, and marked with every evil passion, was turned from one to the other of us, while his deep-set, bile-shot eyes, and his high, thin, fleshless nose, gave him somewhat the resemblance to a fierce old bird of prey.

'Which of you is Holmes?' asked this apparition.

'My name, sir; but you have the advantage of me,' said my companion quietly.

'I am Dr Grimesby Roylott, of Stoke Moran.'

'Indeed, Doctor,' said Holmes blandly. 'Pray take a seat.'

'I will do nothing of the kind. My stepdaughter has been here. I have traced her. What has she been saying to you?'

'It is a little cold for the time of the year,' said Holmes.

'What has she been saying to you?' screamed the old man furiously.

'But I have heard that the crocuses promise well,' continued my companion imperturbably.

'Ha! You put me off, do you?' said our new visitor, taking a step forward and shaking his hunting-crop. 'I know you, you scoundrel! I have heard of you before. You are Holmes, the meddler.'

My friend smiled.

'Holmes, the busybody!'

His smiled broadened.

'Holmes, the Scotland Yard Jack-in-office!'

Holmes chuckled heartily. 'Your conversation is most entertaining,' said he. 'When you go out close the door, for there is a decided draught.'

'I will go when I have said my say. Don't you dare to meddle with my affairs. I know that Miss Stoner has been here. I traced her! I am a dangerous man to fall foul of! See here.' He stepped swiftly forward, seized the poker, and bent it into a curve with his huge brown hands.

'See that you keep yourself out of my grip,' he snarled, and hurling the twisted poker into the fireplace he strode out of the room.

'He seems a very amiable person,' said Holmes, laughing. 'I am not quite so bulky, but if he had remained I might have shown him that my grip was not much more feeble than his own.' As he spoke he picked up the steel poker and, with a sudden effort, straightened it out again.

'Fancy his having the insolence to confound me with the official detective force! This incident gives zest to our investigation, however, and I only trust that our little friend will not suffer from her imprudence in allowing this brute to trace her. And now, Watson, we shall order breakfast, and afterwards I shall walk down to Doctors' Commons, where I hope to get some data which may help us in this matter.'

It was nearly one o'clock when Sherlock Holmes returned from his excursion. He held in his hand a sheet of blue paper, scrawled over with notes and figures.

'I have seen the will of the deceased wife,' said he. 'To determine its exact meaning I have been obliged to work out the present prices of the investments with which it is concerned. The total income, which at the time of the wife's death was little short of 1100 pounds, is now, through the fall in agricultural prices, not more than 750 pounds. Each daughter can claim an income of 250 pounds, in case of marriage. It is evident, therefore, that if both girls had married, this beauty would have had a mere pittance, while even one of them would cripple him to a very serious extent. My morning's work has not been wasted, since it has proved that he has the very strongest motives for standing in the way of anything of the sort. And now, Watson, this is too serious for dawdling, especially as the old man is aware that we are interesting ourselves in his affairs; so if you are ready, we shall call a cab and drive to Waterloo. I should be very much obliged if you would slip your revolver into your pocket. An Eley's No. 2 is an excellent argument with gentlemen who can twist steel pokers into knots. That and a tooth-brush are, I think, all that we need.'

At Waterloo we were fortunate in catching a train for Leatherhead, where we hired a trap at the station inn and drove for four or five miles through the lovely Surrey lanes. It was a perfect day, with a bright sun and a few fleecy clouds in the heavens. The trees and wayside hedges were just throwing out their first green shoots, and the air was full of the pleasant smell of the moist earth. To me at least there was a strange contrast between the sweet promise of the spring and this sinister quest upon which were engaged. My companion sat in the front of the trap, his arms folded, his hat pulled down over his eyes, and his chin sunk upon his breast, buried in the deepest thought. Suddenly, however, he started, tapped me on the shoulder, and pointed over the meadows.

'Look there!' said he.

A heavily timbered park stretched up in a gentle slope, thickening to a grove at the highest point. From amid the branches there jutted out the gray gables and high roof-tree of a very old mansion.

'Stoke Moran?' said he.

'Yes, sir, that be the house of Dr Grimesby Roylott,' remarked the driver.

'There is some building going on there,' said Holmes; 'that is where we are going.'

'There's the village,' said the driver, pointing to a cluster of roofs some distance to the left; 'but if you want to get to the house, you'll find it shorter to get over this stile, and so by the foot-path over the fields. There it is, where the lady is walking.'

'And the lady, I fancy, is Miss Stoner,' observed Holmes, shading his eyes. 'Yes, I think we had better do as you suggest.'

We got off, paid our fare, and the trap rattled back on its way to Leatherhead.

'I thought it as well,' said Holmes as we climbed the stile, 'that this fellow should think we had come here as architects, or on some definite business. It may stop his gossip. Good-afternoon, Miss Stoner. You see that we have been as good as our word.'

Our client of the morning had hurried forward to meet us with a face which spoke her joy. 'I have been waiting so eagerly for you,' she cried, shaking hands with us warmly. 'All has turned out splendidly. Dr Roylott has gone to town, and it is unlikely that he will be back before evening.'

'We have had the pleasure of making the doctor's acquaintance,' said Holmes, and in a few words he sketched out what had occurred. Miss Stoner turned white to the lips as she listened.

'Good heavens!' she cried, 'he has followed me, then.'

'So it appears.'

'He is so cunning that I never know when I am safe from him. What will he say when he returns?'

'He must guard himself, for he may find that there is someone more cunning than himself upon his track. You must lock yourself up from him to-night. If he is violent, we shall take you away to your aunt's at Harrow. Now, we must make the best use of our time, so kindly take us at once to the rooms which we are to examine.'

The building was of grey, lichen-blotched stone, with a high central portion and two curving wings, like the claws of a crab, thrown out on each side. In one of these wings the windows were broken and blocked with wooden boards, while the roof was partly caved in, a picture of ruin. The central portion was in little better repair, but the right-hand block was comparatively modern, and the blinds in the windows, with the blue smoke curling up from the chimneys, showed that this was where the family resided. Some scaffolding had been erected against the end wall, and the stone-work had been broken into, but there were no signs of any workmen at the moment of our visit. Holmes walked slowly up and down the ill-trimmed lawn and examined with deep attention the outsides of the windows.

'This, I take it, belongs to the room in which you used to sleep, the centre one to your sister's, and the one next to the main building to Dr Roylott's chamber?'

'Exactly so. But I am now sleeping in the middle one.'

'Pending the alterations, as I understand. By the way, there does not seem to be any very pressing need for repairs at that end wall.'

'There were none. I believe that it was an excuse to move me from my room.'

'Ah! that is suggestive. Now, on the other side of this narrow wing runs the corridor from which these three rooms open. There are windows in it, of course?'

'Yes, but very small ones. Too narrow for anyone to pass through.'

'As you both locked your doors at night, your rooms were unapproachable from that side. Now, would you have the kindness to go into your room and bar your shutters?'

Miss Stoner did so, and Holmes, after a careful examination through the open window, endeavoured in every way to force the shutter open, but without success. There was no slit through which a knife could be passed to raise the bar. Then with his lens he tested the hinges, but they were of solid iron, built firmly into the massive masonry. 'Hum!' said he, scratching his chin in some perplexity, 'my theory certainly presents some difficulties. No one could pass these shutters if they were bolted. Well, we shall see if the inside throws any light upon the matter.'

A small side door led into the whitewashed corridor from which the three bedrooms opened. Holmes refused to examine the third chamber, so we passed at once to the second, that in which Miss Stoner was now sleeping, and in which her sister had met with her fate. It was a homely little room, with a low ceiling and a gaping fireplace, after the fashion of old country-houses. A brown chest of drawers stood in one corner, a narrow white-counterpaned bed in another, and a dressing-table on the left-hand side of the window. These articles, with two small wicker-work chairs, made up all the furniture in the room save for a square of Wilton carpet in the centre. The boards round and the panelling of the walls were of brown, worm-eaten oak, so old and discoloured that it may have dated from the original building of the house. Holmes drew one of the chairs into a corner and sat silent, while his eyes travelled round and round and up and down, taking in every detail of the apartment.

'Where does that bell communicate with?' he asked at last pointing to a thick bell-rope which hung down beside the bed, the tassel actually lying upon the pillow.

'It goes to the housekeeper's room.'

'It looks newer than the other things?'

'Yes, it was only put there a couple of years ago.'

'Your sister asked for it, I suppose?'

'No, I never heard of her using it. We used always to get what we wanted for ourselves.'

'Indeed, it seemed unnecessary to put so nice a bell-pull there. You will excuse me for a few minutes while I satisfy myself as to this floor.' He threw himself down upon his face with his lens in his hand and crawled swiftly backward and forward, examining minutely the cracks between the boards. Then he did the same with the wood-work with which the chamber was panelled. He walked over to the bed and spent some time in staring at it and in running his eye up and down the wall. He took the bell-rope in his hand and gave it a brisk tug.

'Why, it's a dummy,' said he.

'Won't it ring?'

'No, it is not even attached to a wire. This is very interesting. You can see now that it is fastened to a hook just above where the little opening for the ventilator is.'

'How very absurd! I never noticed that before.'

'Very strange!' muttered Holmes, pulling at the rope. 'There are one or two very singular points about this room. For example, what a fool a builder must be to open a ventilator into another room, when, with the same trouble, he might have communicated with the outside air!'

'That is also quite modern,' said the lady.

'Done about the same time as the bell-rope?' remarked Holmes.

'Yes, there were several little changes carried out about that time.'

'They seem to have been of a most interesting character – dummy bell-ropes, and ventilators which do not ventilate. With your permission, Miss Stoner, we shall now carry our researches into the inner apartment.'

Dr Grimesby Roylott's chamber was larger than that of his stepdaughter, but was as plainly furnished. A camp-bed, a small wooden shelf full of books, mostly of a technical character, an armchair beside the bed, a plain wooden chair against the wall, a round table and a large iron safe were the principal things which met the eye. Holmes walked slowly round and examined each and all of them with the keenest interest.

'What's in here?' he asked, tapping the safe.

'My stepfather's business papers.'

'Oh! you have seen inside, then?'

'Only once, some years ago. I remember that it was full of papers.'

'There isn't a cat in it, for example?'

'No. What a strange idea!'

'Well, look at this!' He took up a small saucer of milk which stood on the top of it.

'No; we don't keep a cat. But there is a cheetah and a baboon.'

'Ah, yes, of course! Well, a cheetah is just a big cat, and yet a saucer of milk does not go very far in satisfying its wants, I daresay. There is one point which I should wish to determine.' He squatted down in front of the wooden chair and examined the seat of it with the greatest attention.

'Thank you. That is quite settled,' said he, rising and putting his lens in his pocket. 'Hello! Here is something interesting!'

The object which had caught his eye was a small dog lash hung on one corner of the bed. The lash, however, was curled upon itself and tied so as to make a loop of whipcord.

'What do you make of that, Watson?'

'It's a common enough lash. But I don't know why it should be tied.'

'That is not quite so common, is it? Ah, me! it's a wicked world, and when a clever man turns his brains to crime it is the worst of all. I think that I have seen enough now, Miss Stoner, and with your permission we shall walk out upon the lawn.'

I had never seen my friend's face so grim or his brow so dark as it was when we turned from the scene of this investigation. We had walked several times up and down the lawn, neither Miss Stoner nor myself liking to break in upon his thoughts before he roused himself from his reverie.

'It is very essential, Miss Stoner,' said he, 'that you should absolutely follow my advice in every respect.'

'I shall most certainly do so.'

'The matter is too serious for any hesitation. Your life may depend upon your compliance.'

'I assure you that I am in your hands.'

'In the first place, both my friend and I must spend the night in your room.'

Both Miss Stoner and I gazed at him in astonishment.

'Yes, it must be so. Let me explain. I believe that that is the village inn over there?'

'Yes, that is the Crown.'

'Very good. Your windows would be visible from there?'

'Certainly.'

'You must confine yourself to your room, on pretence of a headache, when your stepfather comes back. Then when you hear him retire for the night, you must open the shutters of your window, undo the hasp, put your lamp there as a signal to us, and then withdraw quietly with everything which you are likely to want into the room which you used to occupy. I have no doubt that, in spite of the repairs, you could manage there for one night.'

'Oh, yes, easily.'

'The rest you will leave in our hands.'

'But what will you do?'

'We shall spend the night in your room, and we shall investigate the cause of this noise which has disturbed you.'

'I believe, Mr Holmes, that you have already made up your mind,' said Miss Stoner, laying her hand upon my companion's sleeve.

'Perhaps I have.'

'Then, for pity's sake, tell me what was the cause of my sister's death.'

'I should prefer to have clearer proofs before I speak.'

'You can at least tell me whether my own thought is correct, and if she died from some sudden fright.'

'No, I do not think so. I think that there was probably some more tangible cause. And now, Miss Stoner, we must leave you for if Dr Roylott returned and saw us our journey would be in vain. Good-bye, and be brave, for if you will do what I have told you you may rest assured that we shall soon drive away the dangers that threaten you.'

Sherlock Holmes and I had no difficulty in engaging a bedroom and sitting-room at the Crown Inn. They were on the upper floor, and from our window we could command a view of the avenue gate, and of the inhabited wing of Stoke Moran Manor House. At dusk we saw Dr Grimesby Roylott drive past, his huge form looming up beside the little figure of the lad who drove him. The boy had some slight difficulty in undoing the heavy iron gates, and we heard the hoarse roar of the doctor's voice and saw the fury with which he shook his clinched fists at him. The trap drove on, and a few minutes later we saw a sudden light spring up among the trees as the lamp was lit in one of the sitting-rooms.

'Do you know, Watson,' said Holmes as we sat together in the gathering darkness, 'I have really some scruples as to taking you to-night. There is a distinct element of danger.'

'Can I be of assistance?'

'Your presence might be invaluable.'

'Then I shall certainly come.'

'It is very kind of you.'

'You speak of danger. You have evidently seen more in these rooms than was visible to me.'

'No, but I fancy that I may have deduced a little more. I imagine that you saw all that I did.' .

'I saw nothing remarkable save the bell-rope, and what purpose that could answer I confess is more than I can imagine.'

'You saw the ventilator, too?'

'Yes, but I do not think that it is such a very unusual thing to have a small opening between two rooms. It was so small that a rat could hardly pass through.'

'I knew that we should find a ventilator before ever we came to Stoke Moran.'

'My dear Holmes!'

'Oh, yes, I did. You remember in her statement she said that her sister could smell Dr Roylott's cigar. Now, of course that suggested at once that there must be a communication between the two rooms. It could only be a small one, or it would have been remarked upon at the coroner's inquiry. I deduced a ventilator.'

'But what harm can there be in that?'

'Well, there is at least a curious coincidence of dates. A ventilator is made, a cord is hung, and a lady who sleeps in the bed dies. Does not that strike you?'

'I cannot as yet see any connection.'

'Did you observe anything very peculiar about that bed?'

'No.'

'It was clamped to the floor. Did you ever see a bed fastened like that before?'

'I cannot say that I have.'

'The lady could not move her bed. It must always be in the same relative position to the ventilator and to the rope – or so we may call it, since it was clearly never meant for a bell-pull.'

'Holmes,' I cried, 'I seem to see dimly what you are hinting at. We are only just in time to prevent some subtle and horrible crime.'

'Subtle enough and horrible enough. When a doctor does go wrong he is the first of criminals. He has nerve and he has knowledge. Palmer and Pritchard were among the heads of their profession. This man strikes even deeper, but I think, Watson, that we shall be able to strike deeper still. But we shall have horrors enough before the night is over; for goodness' sake let us have a quiet pipe and turn our minds for a few hours to something more cheerful.'

About nine o'clock the light among the trees was extinguished, and all was dark in the direction of the Manor House. Two hours passed slowly away, and then, suddenly, just at the stroke of eleven, a single bright light shone out right in front of us.

'That is our signal,' said Holmes, springing to his feet; 'it comes from the middle window.'

As we passed out he exchanged a few words with the landlord, explaining that we were going on a late visit to an acquaintance, and that it was possible that we might spend the night there. A moment later we were out on the dark road, a chill wind blowing in our faces, and one yellow light twinkling in front of us through the gloom to guide us on our sombre errand.

There was little difficulty in entering the grounds, for unrepaired breaches gaped in the old park wall. Making our way among the trees, we reached the lawn, crossed it, and were about to enter through the window when out from a clump of laurel bushes there darted what seemed to be a hideous and distorted child, who threw itself upon the grass with writhing limbs and then ran swiftly across the lawn into the darkness.

'My God!' I whispered; 'did you see it?'

Holmes was for the moment as startled as I. His hand closed like a vice upon my wrist in his agitation. Then he broke into a low laugh and put his lips to my ear.

'It is a nice household,' he murmured. 'That is the baboon.'

I had forgotten the strange pets which the doctor affected. There was a cheetah, too; perhaps we might find it upon our shoulders at any moment. I confess that I felt easier in my mind when, after following Holmes's example and slipping off my shoes, I found myself inside the bedroom. My companion noiselessly closed the shutters, moved the lamp onto the table, and cast his eyes round the room. All was as we had seen it in the daytime. Then creeping up to me and making a trumpet of his hand, he whispered into my ear again so gently that it was all that I could do to distinguish the words:

'The least sound would be fatal to our plans.'

I nodded to show that I had heard.

'We must sit without light. He would see it through the ventilator.'

I nodded again.

'Do not go asleep; your very life may depend upon it. Have your pistol ready in case we should need it. I will sit on the side of the bed, and you in that chair.'

I took out my revolver and laid it on the corner of the table.

Holmes had brought up a long thin cane, and this he placed upon the bed beside him. By it he laid the box of matches and the stump of a candle. Then he turned down the lamp, and we were left in darkness.

How shall I ever forget that dreadful vigil? I could not hear a sound, not even the drawing of a breath, and yet I knew that my companion sat open-eyed, within a few feet of me, in the same state of nervous tension in which I was myself. The shutters cut off the least ray of light, and we waited in absolute darkness.

From outside came the occasional cry of a night-bird, and once at our very window a long drawn catlike whine, which told us that the cheetah was indeed at liberty. Far away we could hear the deep tones of the parish clock, which boomed out every quarter of an hour. How long they seemed, those quarters! Twelve struck, and one and two and three, and still we sat waiting silently for whatever might befall.

Suddenly there was the momentary gleam of a light up in the direction of the ventilator, which vanished immediately, but was succeeded by a strong smell of burning oil and heated metal. Someone in the next room had lit a dark-lantern. I heard a gentle sound of movement, and then all was silent once more, though the smell grew stronger. For half an hour I sat with straining ears. Then suddenly another sound became audible – a very gentle, soothing sound, like that of a small jet of steam escaping continually from a kettle. The instant that we heard it, Holmes sprang from the bed, struck a match, and lashed furiously with his cane at the bell-pull.

'You see it, Watson?' he yelled. 'You see it?'

But I saw nothing. At the moment when Holmes struck the light I heard a low, clear whistle, but the sudden glare flashing into my weary eyes made it impossible for me to tell what it was at which my friend lashed so savagely. I could, however, see that his face was deadly pale and filled with horror and loathing. He had ceased to strike and was gazing up at the ventilator when suddenly there broke from the silence of the night the most horrible cry to which I have ever listened. It swelled up louder and louder, a hoarse yell of pain and fear and anger all mingled in the one dreadful shriek. They say that away down in the village, and even in the distant parsonage, that cry raised the sleepers from their beds. It struck cold to our hearts, and I stood gazing at Holmes, and he at me, until the last echoes of it had died away into the silence from which it rose.

'What can it mean?' I gasped.

'It means that it is all over,' Holmes answered. 'And

perhaps, after all, it is for the best. Take your pistol, and we will enter Dr Roylott's room.'

With a grave face he lit the lamp and led the way down the corridor. Twice he struck at the chamber door without any reply from within. Then he turned the handle and entered, I at his heels, with the cocked pistol in my hand.

It was a singular sight which met our eyes. On the table stood a dark-lantern with the shutter half open, throwing a brilliant beam of light upon the iron safe, the door of which was ajar. Beside this table, on the wooden chair, sat Dr Grimesby Roylott clad in a long grey dressing-gown, his bare ankles protruding beneath, and his feet thrust into red heelless Turkish slippers. Across his lap lay the short stock with the long lash which we had noticed during the day. His chin was cocked upward and his eyes were fixed in a dreadful, rigid stare at the corner of the ceiling. Round his brow he had a peculiar yellow band, with brownish speckles, which seemed to be bound tightly round his head. As we entered he made neither sound nor motion.

'The band! The speckled band!' whispered Holmes.

I took a step forward. In an instant his strange headgear began to move, and there reared itself from among his hair the squat diamond-shaped head and puffed neck of a loathsome serpent.

'It is a swamp adder!' cried Holmes; 'the deadliest snake in India. He has died within ten seconds of being bitten. Violence does, in truth, recoil upon the violent, and the schemer falls into the pit which he digs for another. Let us thrust this creature back into its den, and we can then remove

Miss Stoner to some place of shelter and let the county police know what has happened.'

As he spoke he drew the dog-whip swiftly from the dead man's lap, and throwing the noose round the reptile's neck he drew it from its horrid perch and, carrying it at arm's length, threw it into the iron safe, which he closed upon it.

Such are the true facts of the death of Dr Grimesby Roylott, of Stoke Moran. It is not necessary that I should prolong a narrative which has already run to too great a length by telling how we broke the sad news to the terrified girl, how we conveyed her by the morning train to the care of her good aunt at Harrow, of how the slow process of official inquiry came to the conclusion that the doctor met his fate while indiscreetly playing with a dangerous pet. The little which I had yet to learn of the case was told me by Sherlock Holmes as we travelled back next day.

'I had,' said he, 'come to an entirely erroneous conclusion which shows, my dear Watson, how dangerous it always is to reason from insufficient data. The presence of the gypsies, and the use of the word "band," which was used by the poor girl, no doubt to explain the appearance which she had caught a hurried glimpse of by the light of her match, were sufficient to put me upon an entirely wrong scent. I can only claim the merit that I instantly reconsidered my position when, however, it became clear to me that whatever danger threatened an occupant of the room could not come either from the window or the door. My attention was speedily drawn, as I have already remarked to you, to this ventilator, and to the bell-rope which hung down to the bed. The discovery that this was a dummy, and that the bed was clamped to the floor, instantly gave rise to the suspicion that the rope was there as a bridge for something passing through the hole and coming to the bed. The idea of a snake instantly occurred to me, and when I coupled it with my knowledge that the doctor was furnished with a supply of creatures from India, I felt that I was probably on the right track. The idea of using a form of poison which could not possibly be discovered by any chemical test was just such a one as would occur to a clever and ruthless man who had had an Eastern training. The rapidity with which such a poison would take effect would also, from his point of view, be an advantage. It would be a sharp-eyed coroner, indeed, who could distinguish the two little dark punctures which would show where the poison fangs had done their work. Then I thought of the whistle. Of course he must recall the snake before the morning light revealed it to the victim. He had trained it, probably by the use of the milk which we saw, to return to him when summoned. He would put it through this ventilator at the hour that he thought best, with the certainty that it would crawl down the rope and land on the bed. It might or might not bite the occupant, perhaps she might escape every night for a week, but sooner or later she must fall a victim.

'I had come to these conclusions before ever I had entered his room. An inspection of his chair showed me that he had been in the habit of standing on it, which of course would be necessary in order that he should reach the ventilator. The sight of the safe, the saucer of milk, and the loop of whipcord were enough to finally dispel any doubts which may have remained. The metallic clang heard by Miss Stoner was obviously caused by her stepfather hastily closing the door of his safe upon its terrible occupant. Having once made up my mind, you know the steps which I took in order to put the matter to the proof. I heard the creature hiss as I have no doubt that you did also, and I instantly lit the light and attacked it.'

'With the result of driving it through the ventilator.'

'And also with the result of causing it to turn upon its master at the other side. Some of the blows of my cane came home and roused its snakish temper, so that it flew upon the first person it saw. In this way I am no doubt indirectly responsible for Dr Grimesby Roylott's death, and I cannot say that it is likely to weigh very heavily upon my conscience.'

Further reading

Face by Benjamin Zephaniah (Bloomsbury Children's Books, 1999)
The central character in this book is on the fringes of a dangerous gang. Then his world is turned upside down after a dreadful accident. He learns that people often judge you by how you look and only true friends can look beyond that.

Northern Lights by Philip Pullman (Scholastic Point, 1998)
The first book in a trilogy about a parallel world where people have their animal daemons to look after them. A world of darkness and danger packed full of adventures.

The Machine Gunners by Robert Westall (Macmillan Children's Books, 2001)
The famous wartime novel by the writer of *Gifts from the Sea*. When Chas finds a German aircraft and machine gun which has crashed near where he lives, the adventures really start to happen.

The Big Football Frenzy by Rob Childs (Corgi, 2000)
A superb collection of three exciting football stories written by the excellent Rob Childs.

Pig Heart Boy by Malorie Blackman (Corgi, 1999)
A book full of issues. A young boy has to face up to a major operation. Animal rights and medical issues are dramatically played out in this thought-provoking book.

Stone Cold by Robert Swindells (Puffin, 1995)
Homelessness is tackled head on in this gritty and tragic novel, which shows just how dangerous life can be if you run away from home.

Suffering Scientists by Nick Arnold (Scholastic Hippo, 2000)
A humorous and fascinating non-fiction book. Any scientist you care to think about is in this book and all sorts of others you haven't heard of!

Programme of study

Each of the following tasks will help pupils to understand the different ways an author's choice of language and structural devices can enhance meaning, convey settings, develop characters and create different moods. Each task is set within the context of one of the stories in this selection, or asks pupils to compare and contrast two or more stories.

Word and sentence

Prefixes

In this task you will look at prefixes and consider the ways in which they can be used.

1. a) Read the first ten pages of *The Speckled Band* quickly and pick out words with the prefixes listed below. Copy out the chart and add the words you have found.

un	con	ex	in
unusual	considerable	excitement	investigation

Look at the words you have found. Which would still be recognisable as proper words without their prefixes? Do they all have the same prefix? Can you invent a spelling rule to help you remember them?

b) Add to the list any other words that use the prefixes listed above. Use a dictionary to help if necessary.

Contractions

In this task you will look at the contractions used in *Under the Ice* and match them to the full form of the word.

2. In pairs, write the following contractions each on a separate card: I'll, I'd, don't, he's, that's, didn't, and any others you can find in the story. Then write the word in full on a new set of cards (for example: I will, I would, do not, he is, etc.). Put the pile of cards of the words in full in the middle of the table face down. Then deal out the contraction cards equally between both players. Turn over the top card of the words in full pile. The first player to match the words in full card with the correct contraction card wins the pair. The winner is the one who wins all the cards.

In this task you will consider the different reasons why authors use contractions.

3. Compare the contractions in *Mayday!*, *Charlotte's Wanderers* and *Rats* by copying out the table below and completing it.

Story	Contractions	Reasons contractions are used
Mayday!		
Charlotte's Wanderers		
Rats		

Dialect

In this task you will look at dialect and consider the ways in which authors use it to create a sense of place.

4. a) Pick out dialect words from *Gifts from the Sea* (which is set in the north-east of England), *The Mouth-organ Boys* (set in the West Indies) and *Fathers' Day* (set in the USA) and try to find out their meanings.

  b) Collect any dialect words you know. They could be words and phrases you only speak to your friends, vocabulary which is local to where you live, or words from another area or country.

Verbs
In this task you will look at verbs and consider how they can add to the impact of a description.

5. Pick out the verbs in the following passage from *Going Up* and explain how each one helps to add to the sense of danger in the description of the fight. The first verb is highlighted for you.

A guy **charged** over a sea of broken glass, aimed a kick at a youth in the doorway and the pair of them swayed snarling out of sight. I slipped off the bench and ran to the door, yelling for my brother. Two police cars stood at the kerb, blue lights flashing. The fight was a few metres away down the street. A woman somewhere screamed.

Adjectives, adverbs and descriptive language
In this task you will look at adverbs and adjectives and other kinds of descriptive language, and consider how they can be used to create different effects for the reader.

6. a) Copy out and complete the beginning of *Seize the Fire* given below, filling in the gaps with words of your own.

Toke _____ his feet as _____ as he could on the forest floor. But, as _____ as each step was on the _____ leaves, he knew that his walk was being _____ by even

softer footfalls. Every now and _____ he would stop and
_____, but all he could _____ was the _____ of his
own heart and the _____ chittering of monkeys and the
birds.

It was getting dark and soon it would be _____ to see
the path without a torch. But it was warm and _____ as
only a _____ forest can be. There would be many _____
hours before the cool of the _____ of the night. And then
he _____ it. One single _____, alarmingly close. He had
been right about the _____ stalker. The tiger was there.

Copy out and complete the chart with your guesses and the
words used in the story:

Your guess	Word from the text	What effect does each word have?
put	placed	'placed' shows that Toke is being careful, whereas 'put' makes it seem as if he doesn't care where his feet go.

b) Describe an incident where somebody is being followed late
at night. Think carefully about your choice of adjectives and
adverbs to help you to build up the atmosphere.

Sentence structures
In this task you will look at sentence structures and consider how
the length of sentences can differ between a modern story and a
story from a historical period.

7. a) Compare the length of sentences in *The Speckled Band* and
Deserter. How can you tell one of these stories was written a
long time ago and one was written recently?

b) Pick out a lengthy sentence from *The Speckled Band* and try to rewrite it as several shorter sentences.

Key sentences

Key sentences help the reader to understand what the rest of the paragraph will be about. In this task you will look at key sentences and consider how they can be used to create a tense atmosphere.

8. a) Look again at the story *Mayday!*. Complete the table below by picking out the key sentence in each paragraph.

Paragraph 1	
Paragraph 2	
Paragraph 3	

b) Choose three of the key sentences you have picked out and explain how they add to the story's tense and frightening atmosphere.

Speech

In this task you will look at how to set out speech and punctuate it correctly.

9. a) Look at the story *Charlotte's Wanderers*. How does the author of this story set out dialogue? Can you work out any rules for setting out and punctuating speech? Think about:
  • where the speech marks are placed
  • the other punctuation used in dialogue
  • when the author begins a new line.
  b) Write out the following passage from *Charlotte's Wanderers* putting the speech marks and other punctuation in the correct places.

Marie says we should have extra practice I thought you'd help
me
But it's half past eight on a Sunday morning
So
We went down to a bit of waste ground by the scrapyard and
began to kick a ball about
We've got to work ... at the ... midfield linkage said Charlotte
between kicks Not getting caught ... in the ... offside trap ...
that's what Marie tells us ... in her team talk
I trapped the ball hard with my foot
Talk is OK I said But ...
But what
I spun round with the ball at my feet Charlotte started to kick at
my ankles trying to hit the ball away
Talk is OK I repeated but it's skill that counts

Text
Use words and phrases from the text to support your ideas in the
following tasks.

1. How are parents and other adults described in these stories? Can
you classify them into types? Which adult characters do you find
sympathetic and caring? Which adult characters are described as
ineffectual or absent?

2. Compare and contrast how young women are portrayed in
Charlotte's Wanderers, *Going Up* and *The Speckled Band*.
Choose one woman from each story. You may wish to use the
writing frame on the next page:

Paragraph one – Introduction – Describe each young woman in a sentence.

Paragraph two – Character one – Main points plus a supporting quotation.

Paragraph three – Character two – Main points plus a supporting quotation.

Paragraph four – Character three – Main points plus a supporting quotation.

Paragraph five – Conclusion – Explain how the two modern characters are different from Helen Stoner.

3. Devise your own board game for *Seize the Fire* showing how Toke overcomes obstacles to help Rafi escape. Create a flow chart showing the key points in the story to help you plan your game. Think about the times when Toke progressed in the story, as well as the moments when he could have been caught.

4. Using the ghost and pre-1914 stories in this collection, plan out your own tale of mystery or suspense. Use a spider diagram or mind map to plan out what you are going to include. Choose from some of the following themes or ideas:

- a mysterious setting
- foreboding at the beginning of the story or everything appearing to be fine
- a first-person narrative
- a detective or private investigator
- an innocent victim
- a twist at the end of the story.

5. Compare and contrast the ways in which the main characters in *Rats* and *Under the Ice* react to ghosts and the supernatural. Think about:
- the type of ghost described in each story
- the way the main character in *Rats* reacts to the ghost
- the way the main characters in *Under the Ice* react to the ghost
- any similarities or differences between the characters' feelings about the ghosts in the two stories.

6. Choose two stories from: *Under the Ice, Gifts from the Sea, Rats* and *The Speckled Band*. Compare the settings of the stories, explain how the author sets the scene and decide which one is the most effective. You may wish to use the writing frame below:

Paragraph one – Introduce the basic setting of your chosen two stories in two or three sentences.

Paragraph two – Describe the setting of the first story and explain how the author creates an atmosphere. Use quotations to support your points.

Paragraph three – Do the same for the second story.

Paragraph four – Explain which setting you prefer and give reasons why.

---

7. Using the atmospheric settings in *Under the Ice, Rats, The Speckled Band* and *Deserter* as a guide, invent and describe your own setting for a story. Think about the kind of story your setting would belong to. Is it a ghost story, a war story or something else? Your setting could be a building, a place in the countryside, or any other suitable idea.

8. Think about the stories you have read in this collection. Which two stories do you think have the best beginnings? Are their openings full of suspense, humour or something else? Give reasons for your choices, and pick out any words or phrases which you think are particularly well chosen.

9. Choose your two favourite endings. Do they explain everything or leave unanswered questions? Do you like to have a few loose ends in a story or do you want everything explained clearly? Think about the type of stories your favourite endings belong to.

Glossary

38	**protruded**: stuck out from
	desolate: lonely and bare
39	**liberated**: made free
40	**spume**: sea spray
	tumult: loud noise
	plaintive: sad, pleading
	flurry: sudden burst
	labyrinth: maze of tunnels
43	**tormentor**: someone causing fear or pain
44	**lunged**: moved suddenly
	interlopers: people who don't belong in a place
45	**fleetingly**: for a second
	contempt: no respect
46	**sheer**: very steep
47	**adamant**: determined
	bracing: supporting and steadying
48	**renewed**: returned
	abyss: deep pit
	precariously: unsteadily

Gifts from the Sea

54	**laths**: strips of wood
	joists: timbers
55	**evacuee kids**: children sent from cities to live in the countryside during the Second World War
	destroyers and corvettes: warships
56	**hoist**: raise
	poss-tub: sink for washing clothes
	poss-stick: a pole for beating clothes during washing
57	**omnipotent**: like God, powerful
59	**barnacles**: shellfish which stick to rocks
61	**mummified**: preserved dead animal
	limpets: small shellfish which stick to rocks

111 **gratified**: pleased
   compositions: children's writing
112 **riveted**: fixed
   goaded: upset
   mincing: putting on an act
   acute: accurate
113 **boisterous**: lively
   vaudeville show: variety or pantomime show
   chores: jobs
   diabolically: wickedly
   pulpy: squashed
   plaintively: sadly
   oblivious: unaware

Seize the Fire
117 **paced**: followed
   chittering: chattering
   brindled: patched
118 **conservation**: projects to save endangered animals
   habitats: homes
   regenerated: remade
   footage: video film
120 **artificial insemination**: creating new life artificially
   compound: enclosed area of land
122 **specimen**: example
123 **mystified**: confused
126 **sabotage**: deliberately damaging items
   liberation: setting free
127 **infiltrate**: to become part of an organisation in order to
   spy on it
128 **mediscan**: health check-up
129 **immobilise**: knock out

130 **fluctuation**: changes
aroma: smell
sinuous: muscled
131 **exultation**: joy
explanatory: explaining
132 **consultation**: discussion
bracing: preparing

Rats
135 **ill-proportioned tale**: badly written
pediment: feature at the front of a building
desirous of solitude: wanting to be alone
136 **traverses**: cuts across
pursued: went on
137 **desultory**: aimless
'twarn't: it wasn't
voluble: talkative
consult: look after
paramount: most important
138 **indefensible**: inexcusable
bolster: pillow
counterpane: bedspread
139 **fancy**: imagination
gingerly: nervously
prosaic: dull
tremulous: shaking
futile: useless
pried: looked
140 **reticence**: unwillingness to talk
fly: horse-drawn carriage
142 **a close tongue**: quiet
recollect himself: pull himself together

The Speckled Band
145 **acquirement**: getting
singular: odd
association: friendship
bachelors: single men
pledge: promise
146 **considerable state of excitement**: extremely upset state
deductions: conclusions reached because of logical thought
intuitions: hunches
147 **pitiable state of agitation**: such a state of worry that you would feel sorry for the person
dog-cart: small horse drawn carriage
bewilderment: confusion
148 **at liberty to defray whatever expenses**: free to pay (Sherlock Holmes') expenses
trivial: unimportant
149 **manifold wickedness**: great evil
dissolute and wasteful disposition: careless with money and indulging in immoral acts
an advance: a sum of money
perpetrated: committed
capital sentence: death penalty
morose: miserable, bad tempered
150 **provision that a certain annual sum**: condition that a sum of money to live on every year
152 **seared**: burned
153 **no great consequence**: unimportant
hubbub: noise
155 **notorious**: well known for something bad
156 **allusion**: reference
159 **nocturnal**: night-time
ejaculation: cry

160 **bile:** bitter yellow liquid from the liver that makes eyes red and unhealthy-looking

161 **amiable:** likeable
insolence: rudeness

162 **trap:** horse-drawn carriage

163 **gables:** triangular wooden posts on the front of houses

165 **pending:** during
endeavoured: tried

166 **counterpaned bed:** bed with a bedspread on it

168 **dog lash:** lead

169 **compliance:** doing what I say
confine: keep

171 **scruples:** doubts

174 **vigil:** wait while keeping watch

177 **erroneous:** wrong

Acknowledgements

We are grateful to the following for permission to reproduce copyright material:

Rogers, Coleridge & White Limited for "Seize the Fire" by Mary Hoffman first published in *Tomorrow Never Knows* by Transworld © Mary Hoffman 1999; Jennifer Luithlen Agency and Robert Swindells for his story: "Seize the Fire"; Laura Cecil Literary Agency for "Gifts from the Sea" by Robert Westall from *Demons and Shadows*; Penguin Books Limited for "The Mouth Organ Boys" by James Berry from *A Thief in the Village and other Stories* published by Hamish Hamilton © James Berry 1987; Walker Books Limited for "Under the Ice" by John Gordon from *The Burning Baby* © John Gordon 1992; Wordsworth Editions Limited for "Rats" by M R James from the Wordsworth Classic Series; and John Goodwin for his story "Charlotte's Wanderers".

We have been unable to trace the copyright holders of "Mayday" by Redvers Brandling, "Fathers Day" by Nathaniel Brenchley, "Deserter" by Anthony Masters and "Going Up" by Robert Swindells and we would appreciate any information which would enable us to do so.